PATRICK LEDWELL

The Acorn Press
Charlottetown
2012

P.O. Box 22024
Charlottetown, Prince Edward Island
C1A 9J2
acornpresscanada.com

Printed and Bound in Canada

Digital composite graphics designed and created by Patrick Ledwell

Cover illustration and Anne vs. Potato illustration by Daniel Ledwell

Scenic photography by Lorraine Costello

Design and layout by Matt Reid

Library and Archives Canada Cataloguing in Publication

Ledwell, Patrick, 1973-
    I am an Islander / Patrick Ledwell.

ISBN 978-1-894838-72-6

    1. Ledwell, Patrick, 1973-. 2. Prince Edward Island--Humor. 3. Canadian wit and humor (English)--Prince Edward Island. I. Title.

PS8623.E4324I24 2012   C818'.602   C2012-901104-5

Canada

Canada Council   Conseil des Arts
for the Arts   du Canada

The publisher acknowledges the support of the Government of Canada through the Canada Book Fund of the Department of Canadian Heritage and the Canada Council for the Arts Block Grant Program.

To my loving wife Tara, who always
greets my best hopes with open arms.

To my parents, Carolyn and Frank, who listened while I
drew and talked for my first six years. Thirty years later,
they encouraged me to get back to telling stories.

To my sisters and brothers, Jane, Em, Thom, Dan, and Christian.
Your talents and dedication are inspiring. I feel lucky
to know you and your loved ones.

Introduction

When you drive the shore roads of Prince Edward Island you can't get too far without coming across a spruce tree hanging over a cliff at a 45 degree angle. I like to tell myself the spruce was deadheading for the mainland and then had a change of heart at the last minute. All happening in tree time, of course.

I carry this picture around in my mind wallet. The tall, gangly trunk suspended in midair, pointing out to sea but held in place by a tangle of deep-running roots.

I believe Prince Edward Island is a unique place. I put this theory to the test by living off-Island for a decade. And then I came back. Since then I taught technology at the Island college, met and got married to a wonderful woman, left my job, and started writing.

I Am an Islander is written out of this return home. The title sounds like a confident one. But it is actually more of a mock-heroic battle cry to hold ground, like a tree tilting at the ocean, when the footing sometimes goes to clay beneath me.

I hope this book gives you a sense of being held between two places: the Island and the world outside, staying or leaving, traditional roots and modern values. *I Am an Islander* is an odd patchwork. There are true stories about growing up, pocket guides on marginal topics, social studies slideshows, and half-disguised rants against new technology.

But all are views from the Island. Because the more I get buffeted by new trends, whether it's yoga or global wines or smart phones, the more I find my responses cropping up from weird places in my Island roots.

It's funny to see news about privacy concerns on Facebook, and then realize that I usually get news about other Islanders through good old-fashioned gossip. Best of luck, Facebook, beating Island conversation to the privacy punch.

It's funny to have GPS in my pocket and then to get Island directions based on landmarks that aren't there any more. "Across from the house with the crazy Christmas lights that they knocked down to build the Shoppers" is not a location you can find on Google Earth.

Welcome to a breezy midair place, where you can stick your head into modern currents, and at the same time find yourself awkwardly tethered by an ever-present past.

Some days, all I need do is remember to carry a pen.

Patrick
May 2012

I Am an Islander

My name is Patrick. And I am an Islander.

Once, I went to Toronto — or, as we call it on PEI, the future. Someone in Toronto asked me, "Hey, do you know Joanne and Gerard Gaudet from Summerside?"

And I said, "Of course I do. Except their names are Juh-wanne and Juh-ward Goody. And they're actually from Travellers Rest."

I am an Islander. And I ask my fair share of questions, too.

I'm a card-carrying member of the PEI Right to Know Association. Dedicated to the mission of asking inappropriate personal questions within the first two minutes of talking to anyone. Questions like "How you doin'? When'd you get back? What're you doin' now? How'd you get into that line of work? What're you makin' at that, if you don't mind me askin'? Who'd you have to know to get that job, anyways?"

Or the most important question of them all, "Who's your father?"

I am an Islander. I cannot rest until I know that.

If the *Star Wars* trilogy happened on PEI, I'd have had the whole Luke's father thing figured out in about five minutes. I'd ask a few questions. "Luke Skywalker? Hell, that's Darth Vader's boy. Skywalker's his mother's name. I can tell a Vader. They all have that breathing problem — you can hear them coming a half-click away."

Three movies just to crack that one genealogical nut? G'way with ya.

Oh, when I say "G'way with ya," I don't mean, "Go physically away." I mean, "Come closer. And tell me more about someone who isn't around right now."

I am an Islander.

Nova Scotia sent me a pamphlet claiming they're "shaped by the sea." Well, la-dee-frickin'-dah. I live on an Island that's not just shaped by the sea — it's eroding by the minute. Beat that, Nova Scotia.

I live on a Gentle Island. With gentle breezes, that gently sandblast all the hair off your legs during a gently breezy day at the beach.

The winter's not too bad, if you scrape off your car right. And by right, I mean you take your scraper and scrape out two eyeholes. Not too bad.

That's the unofficial provincial motto. "Not too bad." It captures our optimism that things aren't yet as bad as they're going to get. Just you wait until February, when the wind's blowing up your pantleg and hurting your feelings.

I am an Islander.

When I say I'm coming over at dinnertime, that could mean noon. Or it could mean seven. Or it could mean that I'll arrive at your house any time between noon and seven and still expect you to feed me.

I call fries a "salad." And I call ketchup a "spice."

When I come to your party I may be wearing sweatpants. Don't worry. For your party, I'll wear my fancy ones, with the pockets.

I am an Islander.

Tourists ask me, "Do you live *and* work here year-round?" I say, "Well, those are two separate questions."

I am an Islander.

I don't call that bag you bring to school a "backpack." It's your kitbag. And what's in your kitbag? Not your notebooks. They're called scribblers. Hilroy scribblers. And on the cover is a map of Canada that's missing PEI. I had a geography scribbler that failed to picture my own province.

Good education. Awful good, dear, terrible good. Desperate wicked altogether, wha'.

I am an Islander.

I come from a place with the biggest go-kart track east of Montreal. I come from a place with the warmest waters north of Florida and the coldest waters you've ever felt south of your belt.

I come from the smallest province, with the longest name. You have to say it like we say it here. Prinsh. Edweer. Ahland. All together now — Prinsh Edweer Ahland! Prinshedweerahland!

My name is Patrick, and I am an Islander.

Come! Playin' on My Island

AN ISLAND EXPLANATION

Placid waters. Sloping cliffs. A picturesque lighthouse. What scene could be more peaceful?

But did you know these cliffs are eroding at the rate of a metre per year? This lighthouse is about to take a unplanned tumble right into the Northumberland Strait and could easily bring a couple of unsuspecting sightseers along with it.

Want shorefront property on PEI? Here's a tip. Buy an inexpensive lot across the road, and just wait.

If you're not educated about the lay of the land, Prince Edward Island can be a perilous place.

Consequently, to enlighten and to warn, I've put together the following all-serving Island explanation.

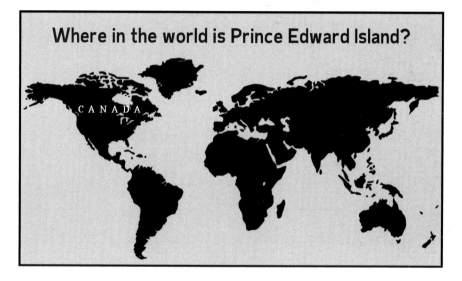

Where in the world is Prince Edward Island?

If you're looking at a map of the world the answer to the above question is: nowhere. The Island is the pregnant pause next to the East Coast comma which is Nova Scotia.

At first, I attempted to draw an arrow indicating Prince Edward Island. But the arrow covered the place where we're not, so I removed it. Useless.

While you're on the Island, do not navigate using a conventional global map. You'll find yourself not only lost, but missing entirely.

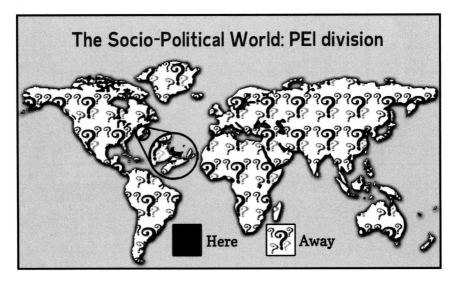

There's a more practical global map in common use on Prince Edward Island. This map divides the world into what we consider two equal halves. One half of the world, shaded in red, is referred to as "Here."

If you overhear an Islander asking after someone, saying, "Is she from Here?" that Islander is asking whether the person is from the red half of the world. And implicitly asking whether the person's umbilical cord was actually cut Here, on Prince Edward Island.

If another Islander replies, "No, she's from Away," that person must be from the remaining half of the world. The "Away" half. That person could be from anywhere in the entire global firmament from Alaska to Australia, an area which we have labelled with question marks.

These Away regions are so labelled because those of us Here are a smidgen unclear as to what's happening in these areas.

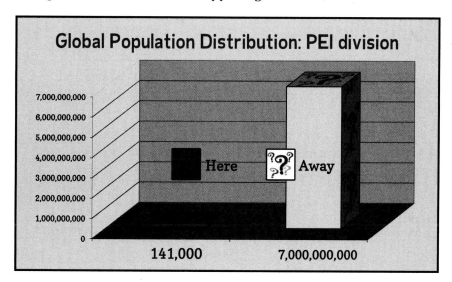

We do have some population numbers, which I received on the provincial fax machine.

The lighter bar on the right side represents those living in the Away regions. Apparently, there are now upwards of seven billion people living Away. People having babies, riding bikes, and quietly doing their business in the morning. The mind truly boggles.

By contrast, the red bar on the left represents those living Here, in Prince Edward Island. That's 141,000 individuals. Bear this in mind. This number must always be factored into your day-to-day conversation Here.

For example, while on PEI never compliment someone by saying, "You're one in a million." We simply do not have the population to back it up. You'll be thought disingenuous, buttering people up like that.

I still remember the magical day when my wife and I proposed to each other on the beautiful North Shore of the Island.

She looked deeply into my eyes and said, "Patrick Ledwell, you are one in one-hundred-forty-one thousand to me. I'd practically have to go over to Moncton to find someone so adequate and still available."

It's that kind of honesty that makes me love her. And this precious place.

SIX IS
ENOUGH

Having a Gander

I grew up on a hobby farm in Prince Edward Island. These days, my more urbane friends ask me, "What do you mean 'hobby farm'?"

The short answer: We ate some of our pets.

Did I feel horrible as a child? Giving human names to animals, like Timothy or Carol, and later re-encountering them in a sandwich?

Nope, not at all.

Nowhere were pangs of regret more absent than with one free-range gander we owned who strutted around under the nom-de-plume "Charlie."

Have you had the misfortune to spend any time close to a gander? The gander is not Mother Nature's finest moment. Start with the cognitive reasoning of a chicken, toss in the anger management of a Rottweiler, and, poof, there it is. Take a gander at that.

Charlie was free in our farmyard to actualize his full potential. As far as I could see, the full potential of a gander is a mission with two simple aims.

The first aim is to convert the entire yard into a minefield of crap. Charlie carpetbombed furiously and equidistantly, until it was impossible for us to pass a soccer ball without it getting redirected by goose globs.

The second aim of a gander in life is to slink up and launch attacks on any moving child.

Charlie was fond of ambushing me when I was already off-balance. It's hard enough for any kid to learn how to drive a bike. It's downright impossible when being buffeted from the flank by a hissing crap factory.

For five years, Charlie subjected me and my five siblings to a farmyard reign of terror, with unprovoked assaults of hissing, pecking, and wing-buffeting. That's 30 years, total, of stolen childhood.

So when it came time for Charlie to meet his planned demise in conjunction with Christmas, we didn't feel horrible at all.

I remember the electric anticipation in the air as all six of us sat, arrayed around the Christmas dinner table, waiting for Charlie the buffeter to get laid out on the buffet table. Tucking the tablecloth into our pyjama tops, banging our forks and knives on the table. Chanting with one voice, from between clenched teeth, "Charlie, Charlie, Charlie! Bring him out, Dad! Bring him out!"

"I call dibs on the wishbone." What's that you wish for, Charlie? Wish you were nicer to me when you were alive? Too late for that now.

A family of piranhas couldn't have picked a goose carcass cleaner than we did that Christmas. My baby brother gnawed for hours on a goose wing and glistened with grease from ear to ear.

What's sauce for the gander is gravy for the babies, Charlie.

I can't imagine any sweeter vengeance than that Christmas scene. Our sworn enemy delivered unto us, roasted on a platter, with his arse stuffed full of bread.

Why I Love Easter

Easter was my favourite holiday as a kid.

At Easter, the Bunny delivers the candy straight to you. Unlike Hallowe'en, when you have to walk all over hell's half-acre picking it up, door-to-door, like a hobo. The Bunny hides the candy, but not that well, and not inside the homes of complete strangers.

And the Easter Bunny doesn't come to town packing Santa's sleighful o' moral baggage. Santa slides down chimneys on a blame spiral, double-checking naughty and nice lists. Really, Santa. I wrote a wish list. I didn't expect an inquisition.

The Easter Bunny, he's not there to judge. Ever hear of the Bunny withholding candy from a kid who's made missteps? Nope, the Bunny gives his chocolate self to everyone and asks for nothing in return.

I grew up in a family with six kids. Space was tight. Budgets probably were too.

A favourite Easter tradition was our trip to the Co-op grocery store with the entire litter packed into a brown Volkswagen Rabbit. What an appropriately named vehicle.

We'd spend the better part of an hour checking out the latest models of Easter bunnies. Some of my siblings went for upmarket models — high-test chocolate, hollow, filled with brand-name candy. I had an eye for heavy, Detroit-style bunnies, with exaggerated haunches like the wheel wells of a Pontiac Parisenne.

The no-name chocolate was not the tastiest ever manufactured, true. But I felt safe because there was lots of it. The Co-op bunnies left a waxy film in my mouth. I'm sure you could have put a wick in one, and it would have burned brightly on the mantelpiece for days.

We'd remember our choices and pile back into the Volkswagen Rabbit, grinning.

I never remember feeling too cramped in the Rabbit. I do remember the ruckus of Easter morning with all of us waking to find the exact model of bunny we'd chosen, a ragtag rabbit squad of different shapes and sizes.

The eating strategies varied. I went on a one-day chocoholic bender. My little brother went all TV serial killer on his bunny. He chopped him into neat cubes and stuck him in the freezer.

The only time I ever regretted having gappy teeth, untouched by orthodontics, was when stealing bites off a sibling's bunny. It was always obviously my chocolate bitemark at the base of a now-missing ear. No need to send it to forensics.

Still, I'd deny the accusations. "Whaaat?" I'd insist. "I can't hear you. And neither can your chocolate bunny anymore."

Instead of getting angry at me, my brothers and sisters should have followed the moral trail blazed by the Easter Bunny.

Because the Bunny is not here to judge. The Bunny is here to forgive. And to give again next year, no questions asked, just like nothing ever happened.

Hand-me-downs

All the pairs of pants I had before the age of 15 were pre-worn velvety smooth before getting to me. They featured a recognizable name on the back — the name of an older American cousin, written in marker on the washing instructions.

We had six kids in my family. And my mother had more than double that number of siblings, a couple of whom had moved to Boston. Likely due to overcrowding. An ideal supply-and-demand system for a cross-border hand-me-down cartel.

At the end of summer, when my American aunts visited, they would plunk down black garbage bags full of hand-me-downs. The parents would root around in the bags and toss each of us a random assortment of cousin cast-offs. We'd nip to the back bathroom and then get frogmarched out to the living room runway for all the adults to judge. A bag-to-school fashion show.

This system presented a sackload of issues. Many clothes were from American colleges, with "Class of '81" insignia that allowed others to pinpoint the exact vintage of the hand-me-downs.

Plus, the clothes were handed down on a "size-first" basis. Gender was a distant, secondary consideration. Especially for my father. He was raised during the 1930s, which permanently stalled his wardrobe development.

"I don't think men play field hockey at Boston College," I'd say, looking downcast at pilly pink gympants whose hips I failed to fill out.

"So they're pink," my father would shoot back, "Who'd be looking at you?"

Oh, mainly the kids with the huge arms, Dad. The ones able to grow moustaches always seem to notice. I was in great aerobic shape that year, dodging them in gym class.

My biggest hand-me-down problem was kicked off by a bright-red New England Patriots jacket. You'd think that an NFL football jacket would be accepted. But in the 1980s nobody at my rural junior high had cable TV, so we were totally ignorant about the New England Patriots, and New England.

The Patriots jacket was a screaming red, with a plush lining blue as a Muppet's pelt. The gigantic logo embroidered on the back was off-putting as well, featuring what seemed to be Ben Franklin playing cornerback in knickers and a three-cornered hat.

"Nice jacket, dork," a moustache-wearer fired off at school. "Who's that on the back? The Quaker Oats Guy?"

"No," I said, "Quakers are pacifists. They don't play football, even." I bet a Quaker could have managed a snappier come-back.

My hand-me-down Patriots jacket made me a walking target — a red, rumpled flack-catcher — and got me forced into a goal-line stand at school.

But I made my first awkward declarations of independence. Somewhere beneath that bright red polyester, I found that I might have my own spirit, handed down from no one.

The PEI Flag

A lopsided woodlot presided over by a huge cougar? What could it all mean?

The PEI flag: If you're in government, it's a shield. If you've just quit high school and got yourself an apartment downtown, it's curtains for you.

But, for all, the PEI flag is majestic, with a handy dotted line on the perimeter that can guide your scissors after you print this image on an old pillowcase. The flag features heraldry symbolizing what happens when a newcomer arrives on the Island. Welcome, friend!

At right, we have the newcomer, represented by the large tree, with its presumptuous foliage and nutty, acorn-like ideas about how to change the place. Note that the Island is small and the new tree is not rooted deeply, so it's not really safe to start swinging around big-feeling branches like that.

At left, we have a more down-to-earth trio of saplings, not growing anywhere but sheltering each other nicely. This cluster represents the close-knit Island community, conspiring among ourselves.

If the flag could show us how the arrival of a newcomer unfolds over time, we'd witness how the close-knit Island community works hard to make the newcomer feel more a part of things. Mainly, by paring back the branching-out to a more manageable level.

The edge on sayings like "Oh, that's different" or "All the power to you" or "How's that working out for you?" might seem a touch dull at first. But if you pay attention, after a while, you'll appreciate their sharpness. Hey, that really cuts! Yee-ouch, I didn't even know I was bleeding.

And the nice thing is the worst is already over by the time the newcomer tree even realizes it's been hacked back to everyone else's level. No sap spilt, very little rustling.

And then nobody is sticking their branches up too far in everybody's face. That's way better, isn't it? Yes, it is.

You'll notice that there is still a distance between the new arrival and the longstanding Island community. This gap will close, rest assured, over the next forty to fifty years, give or take.

This all ties back into our musical Latin motto for the Island, "*Parva sub ingenti.*"

Which translates into English pretty understandably.

Don't go explaining the Latin motto to other Islanders though. That's textbook uppity.

Or then again, all the power to you. Let me know how that works out for you.

Why Anne of Green Gables is a Better Symbol for P.E.I. Than a Potato

VS

Anne of Green Gables vs. the Potato

Some people say potatoes are the symbol for PEI. I don't see it. Potatoes are rough and dirty on the outside and, on the inside, mainly white. Islanders, on the other hand, only have two eyes.

In my abridged PEI dictionary, the word "symbol" is located right between the word "simple" and the word "syphilis." And a good symbol should reflect both its dictionary neighbours.

As a symbol for PEI, Anne of Green Gables is simple enough for both children and Texans to understand. And her cheeriness is more infectious than syphilis. That disease has fallen off in popularity over the last hundred years, whereas Anne has not.

Anne is our beacon to the world, our pre-pubescent Statue of Liberty with braids instead of a spiky headband. She sends the message that you will be welcomed on PEI as long as you have an irrepressible spirit and a fashion sense from the 19th century.

She welcomes to PEI those looking for a simpler age. An age when you could call someone your "bosom buddy" without anyone thinking it's slang for "co-worker with benefits."

When did potatoes ever bring people to PEI? The Irish Potato Famine, that's when. How depressing to run out of what you eat during normal famines.

I have personal experience with the power of the pigtails. I worked at Green Gables House for one endless, nightmarish summer.

I saw people coming from all over the world in Anne drag, wearing straw hats and fake strap-on yarn braids. Fully bearded men wore those braids, not realizing that they looked like the most girlish Vikings ever.

No one arrived with plastic moustaches or interchangeable ears. Because Mr. Potato Head is a child's toy. Anne is a fixation, like the cross-dressing she inspires. Rooted in childhood, but enjoyable life-long.

Americans even think that Anne's real. "Where is Anne buried?" they'd ask. "Oh, deep in your hearts and minds," I'd say.

Visitors got married at Green Gables. And in accordance with PEI laws, some returned years later for Green Gables divorces. Which aren't really divorces but leased farmhouses where couples suffer together in sexless silence for the sake of the children.

Sure, PEI potatoes are famous. The best ones are used as seed and have spread the wide world over. But potatoes are bad role models. I know Island men who spread their seed widely and, unlike potatoes, they aren't considered high quality at all.

Potatoes cannot travel faster than the Green Gables story, which crosses the globe like an imaginative pandemic of A1N2... with an "E."

And it's not just a story. When people come to PEI they still have an experience much like Anne's.

Soon after arriving, Anne dyed her hair the wrong colour, got her bosom buddy too drunk, and fell in love with the one guy she thought she hated, and once smacked over the head. That kind of storybook magic still happens every Saturday night in the streets of Charlottetown.

So give us your dreamy Japanese, your British tourists with their odd sock-and-sandal combinations, your ambiguous bearded men yearning to wear pigtails.

You want change? Go sing in a Toronto subway. Because to quote the musical, Anne of Green Gables will never change. And neither will the Island she so sweetly symbolizes.

SUMMER SHORTS

Choosing the
Perfect Cottage

I've been an expert on cottage life, from an early age.

At seven years old, I figured out why cottage cheese is called that. Normal Cheddar cheese is like our usual house: square-cornered and chock-a-block with rules. Don't just bite off a piece. Were you raised by wolves?

Cottage cheese is like the cottage. Nothing is set and the rules are in chunky flux. Don't like what's for breakfast? Go eat blackened hot dogs, left on the neighbour's grill since last night. Your parents are on vacation, too.

At the cottage, in those days, I slept in my swimsuit and woke up fully dressed for the day. Then straight out the screen door to join a roving pack of children, hair matted like the grassy path between cottages.

I tromped through dozens of different cottages, scavenging with this unsupervised child pack. The cottages all had a few indispensable elements of décor necessary to conjure the right relaxed standards, for kids and parents alike.

So whether you're looking to rent or own, here's my tour of what to look for in the perfect cottage.

Note: These standards have not changed since I learned them in the late seventies. Not changing since the seventies is the core feng-shui principle of the perfect cottage.

Let's make our way through the yard, where the perfect cottage should have at least two items of painted plywood yard art. Some possible themes include "Woman Accidentally Showing Bloomers While Weeding Flowerbed" or the more risqué "Boy Peeing Plastic Yellow Rope." Luckily, years of exposure have peeled away most of the off-colour details.

The living room is where the parents will spend the day. They will be smoking with the orange curtains shut, playing cribbage on a spool-shaped coffee table that once held telephone wire. It now holds conversation-provoking centrepieces, such as a seashell-themed ashtray. Or an actual seashell, serving as an ashtray. Fire and water, balanced. Very feng-shui.

The kitchen is small. It doesn't matter because no one is cooking. The stove's pilot light is too dangerous. Kitchen accessories include a collection of amusing seasoning dispensers, shaped like chubby farm animals, grinning despite their high blood pressure. In Atlantic

Canada, all the containers contain only salt, which will be ancient and stuck in there, solid.

The bedroom just off the hall is spilling over with dog-eared board games, for hours of endless fun. I mean endless, because the games are missing the parts necessary to actually win and complete the game.

The game will last so long you'll need a bathroom break, in the tiny yet cramped cottage bathroom. The toilet will be sweating profusely, probably because it's wearing a shag hat in the summertime.

The bathroom is stocked to the ceiling with everything that nobody needs, like handicrafts. Observe the posted needlepoint philosophy, reminding all sweeties to wipe the seatie. All told, when you're seven, the path of least resistance is to follow the invitation of the plywood boy in the front yard and just go outside.

Which reminds me of my favourite piece of needlepoint philosophy: "The cure for everything is salt water — sweat, tears, or the sea."

There's plenty of time in life spent on the first two. So this summer, get a classic cottage for just a while. Go to bed in your swimsuit and wake up with your hair tousled by dreaming. With the window wide open, and the usual rulebook heaved a safe distance outside.

The Skinny on Summer

Some people are sad to see the last days of summer take wing. Not me. I'm happy when it's over. Because once summer is gone, so too are the circumstances when I need to take off my shirt in public.

In the spring, the covers of my wife's magazines all start to ask the same question: "Is your beach body ready?" This year, I lived through my 38th summer. I'm beginning to suspect that my beach body might never be arriving.

I'm skinny — there's no two ways of looking at it. I mean, there are literally not two ways of looking at me. I'm built like a plasma TV. From the side, I'm relatively featureless.

Even my own family tells me I'm skinny. Especially my aunts at summer reunions. "Are you eating enough?" they say, crossing their arms across their farm-built torsos, solid as peat-moss outbuildings. "I just talked to your beautiful wife. Didn't you do well for yourself?"

I can hear what they mean by that. "Patrick, weren't you just skinny enough for the blind spot in her judgment, you unsubstantial creature?"

Just because my chest is two-dimensional, that doesn't mean that there isn't a real human heart beating inside it.

And my paper-thin heart is at its most vulnerable when I have to peel off my T-shirt at the beach. I glance at my highly proportional wife, lying on a towel. I recall our wedding vows and feel relieved that she's now legally obliged to love what I'm revealing.

For me, it's a regression in life to take off my shirt. It's a public airing of the fact that, beneath my adult veneer, I still possess the bird-chested tentativeness of an ten-year-old boy.

To make matters worse, I lurch into the cold Atlantic ocean with the reluctance of a fully plucked blue heron. My arms go aloft, like fleshy wings, outstretched for a flight they're incapable of taking.

The waterline reaches my drawstring, and that shock hurtles me even further backwards in evolutionary time. I don't even look like a bird anymore. I'm the missing link between dinosaurs and birds. I'm just pale skin stretched over pointy parts, with only enough brain for fight-or-flight responses.

I choose flight from the cold Atlantic, with the unlovely cry of a ptero-dactyl, and I scare children from the water's edge.

So, I'm relieved when I finally see geese gathering on the horizon, suggesting that summer, too, is going south. Thank you, geese, for leaving behind your down for my jackets and vests, which I will layer around my willowy frame until I look like a normal, whole person again.

A Few Signs of Intelligent Life on Prince Edward Island

Here is a sign indicating the big PEI turn-off, from New Brunswick. Another big PEI turn-off is that this is the last traffic sign anyone reads or follows from this point onward. Abandon all road regulations, ye who enter here.

Islanders drive as independently as Quebeckers but without the passion or the purpose. Our loose, interpretive driving style puts the Î.-P.-É. in "Yipe!"

A laissez-faire observance of signs has set our tiny Island on a dangerous collision course. The way we treat crosswalks, you'd swear the white stripes were there just so we could line up the pedestrians better.

It's time for a short refresher course on Island signs.

Let's start with an easy one.

You are in PEI

This sign states the obvious. When you are being cradled on waves of broken pavement, you generally realize it: You are in PEI.

Putting up these signs on the Island is like putting "slippery when wet" warnings all down a waterslide.

The Department of Highways should save considerable time and effort and develop a Smooth Pavement sign. They would need about three.

Perfectly okay to stop & talk across lanes and hold everyone the heck up

This is fairly self-explanatory, too. The circle indicates that it is permitted to do what is pictured.

Still, when encountering two Islanders stopped and talking across lanes, some people persist in honking their horns rudely or making inappropriate gestures. Really. It's clearly permitted in this zone.

Where's the friggin' fire?

Many Islanders enjoy our pedestrian and cycling trail system to get some fresh air, or because the driver's license is still under suspension. When you come to a crossroads on the trail you'll be greeted with this mysterious set of hieroglyphs.

Remember, the circle always indicates what is permitted. It is okay to bike and it is okay to ski.

And it is okay to have your dog spaded.

I haven't solved this last rebus beyond a doubt. Some suggest that it relates somehow to poop-and-scoop bylaws. If your dog needs that style of shovel to pick up its droppings, please exercise caution. Because you appear to have a grizzly bear for a dog.

Now, a difficult one. The sign at left is our most ambiguous wayfinding symbol. It's like a Rorschach inkblot test. Different people see different things in the blob.

When Islanders see this sign, they think, "I don't want to pay for the beach. I'll pull into the kiosk, and lie that I'm just driving around to the harbour to buy fish."

When visiting Americans see this sign, they think, "This way for pork chops."

I worked in a Visitor Information Centre. On a regular basis, U.S. tourists came in and asked, "What's the deal with all the pork chop signs?" They arrived on the North Shore hungry, their carnivorous appetites whipped into a frenzy by the come-hither suggestion of meaty chops.

No wonder the National Park has difficulty protecting endangered shore birds. Americans are eating them, disappointed about the pork chops.

I have no idea what this means. It looks like a recycling sign, and I have no idea how to recycle either.

I'm not alone in my confusion. Observe that two other Islanders have pulled their cars fully off the road onto the grassy area and are mulling over what to do next. "Let's call CAA to tow us home. Because the road appears to have buckled into some sort of loop."

Cropping up across the countryside, these mysterious circles have split families apart and have left some Islanders unable to return to their place of work.

There was only a single time I've ever been glad to see this sign. It was on a very slippery day last winter. Right after passing the sign, I hit black ice and went into a 360-degree spin. So many questions flashed through my mind.

Questions like, "If I'm in a 360, and I hit the traffic circle, will it straighten me out?"

Well, obviously, it did. I survived.

QUICK FIXES FOR THE FECKLESS

Our Heritage Names

If you need time to think, go to a kindergarten graduation.

I went to my niece's daytime graduation from Mary's Little Lambs. Sitting there with my nametag, I watched each child get a certificate, pursued by photo-snapping grandpaparazzi.

Here's what struck me: There was zero crossover between the grand-parents' nametags and the children's nametags.

The grandparents bore the stalwart names that got Canada through the last war — Bertha, Lloyd, Edna, and Herbert. But no grandchildren were bearing these heritage names forward.

The boys' names had the abrasive sound of cleaning supply brands — Jace, Brayden, and Bryson. The girls' names chimed with the promised freedom of urban sport vehicles — Sierra, Jada, and Skylar.

Here's what I want to know: Will heritage names disappear? True, it seems strange to saddle newborns with mid-century monikers like Floyd or Florence. But in the baby's future professional life, will his or her trendy name command the same respect as a sturdy heritage name?

Simple test. Which statement inspires more confidence? "This is your public defender, Skylar Summer Jones," or "This is your defense attorney, Eleanor Eunice Jones." Unanimous decision.

Then, at the never-ending graduation, I was struck with a simple, elegant solution. Right now, parents are picking first names to make the child popular in kindergarten. And they use middle names to hide tributes to Jurassic-era family members with heritage names like Gertude or Wallace.

I hereby propose that Canada create Name Leapfrog Legislation that enacts the following law: When a person turns 25 — hereafter known as their leapfrog year — they will jump to using their middle name in place of their first name, effective automatically. Like drinking age and voting age, a name-change age.

The child can ride the popularity of a trendy name like Brianna or Mikayla while it and she are still fresh and bubbly. Then, at 25, when she's graduating med school, leapfrog time. She can instantly derive the dusty gravity of a heritage name, like Bertha or Myrtle, previously concealed as a middle name.

At the kindergarten graduation, the children were now pinned with letters and arranged into the words "grow" and "learn," and they began to sing. Their sweet singing for the misty-eyed oldsters caused me to reflect, "What's in a name? Maybe a rose by any other name would smell as sweet?"

Then, I snapped to my senses again. "No, that's stupid. It depends on the age."

Gladys is an awesome name for grandma but a damn weird name for a little girl. Support my idea and you can call her Piper G. as a budding youth, and then after 25 years, P. Gladys in the first bloom of her medical career.

Unless she turns out to be an aromatherapist. In which case, Piper would pass the smell test just fine.

Wine Buying for the Non-Wine Buyer

Is it possible to pick a good wine in no time flat? You bet Shiraz. Grab your stemmed goblet and follow me.

1. *Choose winemaker names that sound like bad hockey players.*

In your hockey pool, you pick guys like Gordie, Steve, or Wayne. Lunch-bucket guys. You don't pick Julio or Ernesto because they sound like they're from hot, soccer-playing countries. It's the exact opposite when you choose wine. Never choose a wine called Zinfandel by Gordie.

2. *The dates on wine are the reverse of the dates on milk.*

If you found a milk carton with an old date in your fridge, what would you do? You'd stick your nose into the container, inhale deeply, and carefully judge what you smelled. Maybe take a tiny test sip. Buy some old wine and do the exact same thing as with old milk. Except with wine, people will be impressed.

3. Avoid wines from countries with more than six consonants.

Wines from Argentina (at five consonants) are a fine bargain. Wines from Kyrgyzstan (at nine consonants) are a bitter compromise. You will use those extra "r" and "g" sounds to make unwelcome noises in the morning. Trust me.

4. In its description, a wine should either be compared with a wood or any flavour you would tolerate in a doughnut.

"Full-bodied, with notes of dark cherry"? Yes! Cherry is both a handsome wood and a tasty doughnut.

"Asphalty textures"? No. Wood is the only building material permissible.

"Velvety plum, with tobacco accents"? Okay. Because to be honest, I'd probably still eat that doughnut.

Affectiliate

I've played squash many times with Peter. But I didn't know much about the guy. One day, when he'd said he'd been up late working out a conflict with his new partner Brad, I didn't know how to react.

My wife said that Peter opening up to me about his partner was a significant moment, and that I should recognize it.

So I went to buy some congratulation towels and matched two that were monogrammed "His" and "His." I gave them to Peter after our next game. He looked confused.

The next week, he said he was getting too busy for squash now that he was full partner at his legal firm. Oh, a *legal* partner. He said that his *legal* partner Brad was maybe looking for a new partner. For squash. I think.

Obviously, the word "partner" needs help. Modern living has tasked it with too many jobs and it's managing them poorly. When you're not married and you want to describe your main emotional relationship, "partner" is the least bad of currently available options.

"Lover"? That sounds sordid, like the other person stays at home all day in a crushed velvet bathrobe, eating chocolates. "Special Friend"?

Strictly for obituaries.

And then there's the confusion between forms of partnership. Take a male lawyer — who's a full partner — living with another male lawyer from the same firm — who has not made full partner. Beside the emotional baggage they'd have as lawyers in love, how would one introduce the other at a cocktail party?

"This is my partner Brad, not *legally* my partner yet though." Nice save. But people would probably hear that the speaker was non-committal about same-sex marriage, not that Brad was still articling.

I propose introducing a new word into the English language. A word to replace "partner" in all future relationship references. The word is "affectiliate."

It perfectly harmonizes roles as lovers — through the root "affection" — with the responsibilities of a long-term relationship — through the root "affiliate."

Let's revisit our earlier scenario with the two lawyers at the cocktail party. One could easily say, "This is my *affectiliate* Brad, from the law firm where we both work." Clear? Like crystal.

Affectiliate. If you agree the word would help clear up confusions, well, put 'er there... partner.

I was in line at the grocery store. While waiting, I overheard two older women discussing a mutual friend. "Edna's on The Facebook," one said. Yes, not just any Facebook, but *the* Facebook. "And she's listing her status as 'interested in men.'"

Her friend was quick to answer. "Edna? Interested in men? Imagine!"

"Imagine!" It's a word often overheard on Prince Edward Island as a kind of punctuation accompanying a thought. And it deserves some explanation.

At first, hearing "imagine" may conjure up memories of John Lennon. In his music, that single word evokes a new world of possibilities. A world where people live for today and change is always conceivable.

On PEI, not so much.

Let's examine how the word "imagine" works on the Island. For starters, the word takes a little trip. For John Lennon, the word comes at the start of the sentence, to open up a thought about some fantastical change.

On the Island, "imagine" travels all the way to the end of the idea, to close it off. Plus, it converts that hopeful thought into a question. A question now punctuated with a sharp, "Imagine!"

As if to say, can you imagine anyone in their proper-thinking brain even entertaining that fool notion long enough to utter it?

Can you imagine someone actually saying that and wasting perfectly good air, which is probably the only thing keeping an empty head inflated?

I've heard the word in my travels.

"Leaving a secure public service job, to become some kind of comedian, in Canada's smallest province? Imagine!"

You may say I'm a dreamer. I imagine I'm not the only one.

Poetry Is Self-Indulgent and Irrelevant

Poetry is the writing equivalent of exposing yourself in public: understandable only for the person doing it. And like flashers, poets wear creepy raincoats too often, even when it's not raining.

I have my Masters in English Literature. That's a lot like having your blackbelt in puppetry. I've got lethal skills in an artform no one gives a crap about.

I wasted six years of post-secondary education lazing around in beer-soaked turtlenecks, just to discover that poetry is self-indulgent.

If you actually want to communicate, why spend hours writing poetry in an attic, secretly manipulating your diction? Do not use language that is abstruse and recondite. You will be ostracized. Probably for using words like "ostracized."

Poetry runs in my family like a horrible blood-borne disease.

My father was the poet laureate of Prince Edward Island. Yes, we have one. And laureate must be the Latin word for "paid in potato leaves." Luckily, my father had other interests, such as teaching and not starving his damn family.

Many members of the League of Canadian Poets tramped through my parents' home when I was a child. What a treat. If your home has too much spare alcohol, and not enough wet wool and disappointment, contact your local chapter of the League today to arrange a poet visit.

Most people get the poetry beaten out of them by pointless junior-high classes on the haiku. Not me.

In university, I actually believed my knowledge of Shakespeare's sonnets would get me somewhere. "My mistress' eyes are nothing like the sun," I whispered at the bar, to the girl with the messed-up eyeshadow from creative writing class. Then a football player built like a port-a-potty walked up to her and said, "Me so horny." Guess who left with her?

Poetry hasn't helped me with a single practical thing in life. At the hardware store, I now wander the aisles lonely as a cloud, reciting my memorized William Blake. "What the hammer? What the chain? / Could frame thy fearful symmetry?"

Poetry is a fearful symmetry — a purposeless loop of grief in, grief out. Any rational person should avoid it, especially after seeing its delightful effect on the world's great poets.

Percy Shelley? Drowned like an idiot. Emily Dickinson? Never left the house. Robert Frost? Took the road less travelled by and starved his damn family.

TEENAGE
WASTELAND

High School Choices

1991. My high school graduation. I remember our valedictorian saying, "You'll look back at these years as the best time ever, a time when you made choices that set you on the highway called Life."

She was only half right.

High school was actually a time when poor course choices created deep potholes in my Life highway.

In high school, I was a bookish lad. I was built like a sunflower with a gargantuan head that my stem-like body struggled to support.

Glancing at my weedy physique, my guidance counsellor advised me to take every available science course, even physics, which ruled out fitting phys. ed. in my schedule.

"Okay," I thought, "Who knows more about getting a hot career than a high-school guidance counsellor? Just look at his tiny, windowless office."

Eighteen years later, as a college teacher, I signed up for co-ed staff basketball. Thanks to my physics course, I could always predict where a missed shot was about to ricochet. Guesstimate shot arc, plug in velocity, and solve for the rebound. But could I actually get to where I knew the ball was going? Not powered by my gym-class-dropout physique, so easily boxed out by the other teachers.

Another regret: I went to high school before the personal computer, when you got educated so you didn't have to type. I took art instead. I envisioned myself as a Renaissance bureaucrat, able to dictate off-the-cuff memos, and then retreat to my office to dash off some quick watercolours of birds.

Imagine my shock when the computer made typing a job prerequisite. No employer now values that I can paint up to three watercolour birds per minute.

When I was a teacher at a public college, I endured years of embarrassing hunt-and-peck, my two fingers poised above the keyboard like idiotic, eyeless chickens. I left out the "l" in "public" so many times that I'm through bushing. I mean, blushing.

And finally, at my high school, taking jazz band meant that I didn't have room in my schedule for Grade 11 health class. Otherwise known as "The Facts of Life."

My trumpet solos in "Funny Valentine" won me one or two necking sessions with band girls, who seemed to appreciate my disciplined lip positions. But without a sex ed. textbook, I was completely in the dark about what came next. So I practised "Satin Doll" on my horn. And I resigned myself to the fact that bedroom-wise, I'd just have to give it a whirl, playing it cool as can be.

A trumpet has seven fingerings and about four-and-a-half feet of tubing. Knowing what I know now, if I had to choose either trumpet or human sexuality as a topic to figure out on my own, I know what course I'd take.

Choosing high school courses was like facing two roads diverging in a yellow wood, to quote the poem from English class. High school made me travel only one road, and my Life highway forked from that moment onwards.

All Teens Are Vampires

You'd have to be trapped in a coffin to avoid the *Twilight* saga, these days. Maybe you'd prefer to be.

My wife and I braved a late movie at the googleplex to catch the latest installment of the teen vampire phenomenon. And it was bloody terrible.

I sat for two hours staring blankly at the screen, as vacant as the living dead staring back at me. The dialogue was wooden and drove a stake right through anything I was supposed to feel. "I'm a 104-year-old immortal, but of all possible eras, I've chosen to become an emo boyfriend, mucking through this colour-drained slop trough of neediness and tears."

The teens surrounding us, on the other hand, ate it right up, wooting as a pack when any character whipped his shirt off and changed into a wolf.

I guess I just don't get the *Twilight* saga because I'm not a vampire. And I believe that all teens actually are. Vampires, I mean. That explains why I have such an irrational fear around groups of them, now that I'm in my late thirties.

Evidence of teen vampirism was everywhere in the googleplex. All the teens were ashen-faced and sullen, even without movie makeup. Their hoodies blocked all ambient light, except the bluish glow spilling upwards from their cell phones.

You wouldn't believe the food containers that flew out behind the roiling cloud of teens leaving the theatre. Trans-fats. Processed sugars. People who feed their faces so heedlessly must believe they're going to be living dead forever.

My wife and I were so exhausted after the late movie we barely made it back to the car. The pack of teens twitchily marauded off to the next midnight activity, like born creatures of the night. Don't they realize that they'll be drained and powerless to get up in the morning? Exactly. More proof of vampirism.

Even though it was 20 years ago, I can't remember spending my teenage years roving in such a soulless state.

Sure, I was a drain on my parents like most teens. No car, no money, and not within a country mile of a girlfriend. I was like a hairless pet living at their house. Happy if fed on schedule. Pretty benign.

Extra-curricular activities, that's what saved me. My concert-band sweater was like a staticky protective barrier, rendering me invisible to popular peers who could have offered me recreational drugs, or any form of intimacy whatsoever.

There was that time, though, when I asked the oboe player with the black lipstick to the Christmas dance. She said no. Probably because I caked on too much Clearasil acne coverup that day. Its roast-chicken skintone never seemed to blend with my mashed-potato face.

And so I didn't go to the dance, and my friend found his Dad's stash of Coors Silver Bullet, and we shotgunned it watching *The Lost Boys*, then climbed a TV tower outside town, which could have gotten us killed, but all I could think about was how my infinite sadness somehow needed to be broadcast to the world.

I do remember not getting up until dark the next night, feeling 104 years old, my pallid body sweating out Silver Bullet.

Maybe I've got *Twilight* wrong. What's so bad about teens connecting up their turmoil with a timeless battle between good and evil? If an escapist vampire saga helps them survive high school without turning into complete zombies, it can't be all bad.

Because there's one thing *Twilight* nails about being a teenager — it sucks.

The Island Wooden Clock

This is my Grade 9 Industrial Arts project.

The Island Wooden Clock

What industry was that class preparing me for? The fast-moving wooden-clock industry, I guess. If there is ever a worldwide shortage of liquid quartz, my skills will be in demand.

For decades, Island curriculum experts have deemed it a good idea to have grade niners, jangly with hormones, carve our province out of wood on the jigsaw.

That's a challenging first project, to put it mildly. The Island may be small, but it's a complex geographical shape.

I can remember slaving away at the power equipment as a 15-year-old and complete jigsaw novice. I was trying not to get distracted by girls at the next workstation who were leaning over their ceramics and smoothing still-glistening surfaces with their hands.

I worked so hard to concentrate and get our coastline accurate. Every bay, cove, and inlet. Guiding the jigsaw along the irregular bitemarks of Hillsborough Bay, up around the East Point protrusion, heading West to Malpeque Bay. Like a real Jacques Cartier of the jigsaw.

But I never made it all the way around. I'd always get to the point where the Island gets wicked thin, right around Summerside. My sweaty, puberty-stricken hands would slip, and I would accidentally cut off Prince County. A breakaway county, flying across the shop.

I did that three times trying to complete my Industrial Arts requirements.

Finally, I gave up. I retrieved Prince County and grabbed the remaining Island landmass off the jigsaw. I marched straight to the shop teacher and presented the two chunks.

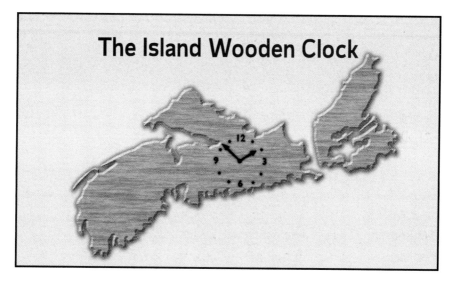

The Island Wooden Clock

"Look, I made Nova Scotia," I said. "This smaller chunk is Cape Breton, and there's the rest of the peninsula. Can I be excused from this class?" Forever, I hope.

Why are Island adolescents set up for failure with this impossible geo-jigsawing challenge?

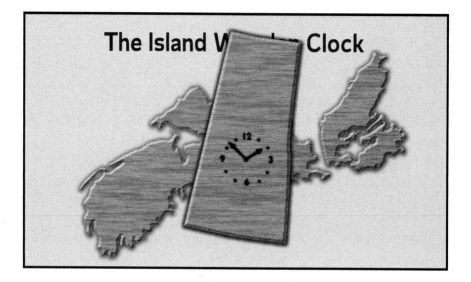

Consider the other provincial clocks in Canada.

In Saskatchewan, all the junior-high students need to do is to saw the end off a two-by-four, stick a clock in it, and they're done. Finished Industrial Arts, forever.

It's not fair.

SOCIAL
NOT-WORKING

Digital Baby Photos

With the explosion of digital cameras and photo sharing, babies are being snapped and uploaded by parent paparazzi during every single waking moment. Oh, wait, there are some of him sleeping, too. So sweet.

If you're like me, after every holiday or significant family event you get hit with a baby boom of digital photos. It's time to advance some guidelines for sharing baby pictures in a digital world.

1. *I shall reduce the size of the baby photos I send.*

There's no need to send me baby photos at ultra megapixel resolution. I'm not printing them for a 20-foot diaper billboard by the freeway.

My sister-in-law sent me a bandwidth-bending e-mail with many gigantic attachments of my nephew. When clicked, the photos popped up so zoomed-in, they could have been views from a space probe exploring a fuzzy peach-coloured planet. I tried to scroll around to find the baby's face but just got a crusty crater of a nostril in the middle of my screen. That's too much data on your little nose-miner, thanks.

2. I shall not use a baby picture as my computer desktop, when my desktop is really messy.

Recently, I borrowed my sister's computer. I gasped to see a smiling picture of my niece on the desktop, except with Microsoft Office documents where her eyes and teeth should be. Like an outbreak of Word-document pox.

You wouldn't staple grocery lists on a baby portrait. Then don't put a baby picture on your pigpen of a desktop.

3. I shall not use my baby's picture as my Facebook profile picture.

I had a high-school reunion over Christmas, all organized on Facebook. I noticed that many former classmates use one of their infant's photos as their profile picture. A close-cropped shot of a newborn can really resemble his disgruntled car-salesman dad. But this still qualifies as stealing the baby's identity, in my books.

It's bad enough to get mocking Facebook comments about my reunion behaviour, and some poor decisions vis-à-vis Jello shooters. But I don't appreciate having some of those comments attributed to a pictured five-month-old.

4. I shall not send my friends every single photo of the cutest baby ever.

I'm getting sent so many photos of some babies that it qualifies as surveillance. Here's a fast way to filter out a few baby pictures: Ask yourself, would this picture still be cute if a 38-year-old man were involved?

Happy baby in a clean outfit, giving a big kiss to a consenting friend? Nice, and also okay for a 38-year-old man.

Baby shirtless and conked out, covered in pink Jello stains? I don't need to delve into that part of baby's life. And anyone with an ounce of compunction would take that picture of me off the Facebook reunion page.

Vaguebooking

Some people get angry when friends share too much information on Facebook. I actually get concerned when people don't give me enough detail in their status updates.

"Jennifer is trying to get through it." Get through what? "Tim will never, never do that again." What did you do, Tim? Time for an intervention, or did you just eat burritos for lunch again?

Purposeful ambiguity has gone so viral on Facebook that there's now a term for it — vaguebooking.

Vaguebooking is the habit of posting indefinite status updates, either as crafty attention-seeking devices, or as barely audible cries for help. Or both. It's difficult to tell.

Last week, I wondered what murky shadow had crept across a set of my college friends who were posting statuses heavy with unclarity and foreboding.

"Take a look at me now. There's just an empty space," updated my former roommate, who now programs software. He used to have some darker times, and I haven't seen him in person for a decade. What's going on? Then, a comment from another friend who does macroeconomics for government: "I've been a prisoner all my life."

"I can feel it coming in the air tonight," posted a third friend, who's now vaguely involved in American TV. I was getting anxious, troubled that my friends might be experiencing tragedy in threes, like celebrities.

"What's coming? You okay?" I commented, a bit concerned. My TV friend fired right back for all to see, "I've got a serious case of the Phil Collinses. He just announced his retirement. Get a grip. Mwah-ha-ha."

With this whiff of context, the source of these once-worrying statuses was now staring me right in the face. As clearly as Phil Collins's huge head used to stare out at me from his LP covers.

So I could have been quicker on the uptake. But seriously, would it kill you to type "— Phil Collins" at the end of your status, so I don't take everything at face value? What are the odds I can identify any unattributed song fragment from the eighties, and tell it apart from someone's genuine emotions?

That's against all odds. And it's the chance I've got to take, I guess, if I ever want to respond to any of you manipulative, indefinite Facebookers, ever again.

So to my vaguebooking friends, some advice. If you can feel it coming in the air tonight, please just tell me what "it" is, so I can respond appropriately, whether it's existential dread or simply the burritos you had for lunch coming back at you.

And if you actually need help, ask me outright. I'll come running, anywhere. To quote Phil Collins, just say the word.

Twitterature

Who gets time to read anymore?

I majored in English literature, but I work with computers now. It's a race against the clock to stay up to date. Making posts on my weblog, revising my on-line profile, or even filling in that little "What are you doing?" box on social networking sites: It all takes doing.

There aren't enough leisure hours left in the day for epic masterpieces.

Luckily, I've discovered a new on-line service that allows me to experience all the great books, packaged for my just-in-time lifestyle. It's called Twitterature.

Twitterature pushes me timeless books using 140 characters or fewer. I'm talking 140 characters in the "140 letters max" sense. Not in the "140 people in the book" sense, like a Tolstoy novel.

If Tolstoy were writing today, he'd realize that he needs to get to the point a lot faster. Twitterature performs the update for him, slicing away fatty exposition to leave behind pure wisdom nuggets.

Okay, I've just added Tolstoy's *Anna Karenina* to my reading list. And here it arrives... Boop! "All :) families are alike; every :(family is :(in its own way." And I'm all done. Delete.

Twitterature has even turned me on to Jane Austen. I used to wonder why anyone alive today would be interested in these rehashings of 18th century marriage plots. *Sense and Sensibility. Pride and Prejudice. Repetition and Redundancy.*

But with Twitterature, I receive entire Jane Austen books through the week, conveniently parcelled into relationship status updates. This week I've been following Elinor@Sense... *Sensibility* doesn't fit in the max characters limit.

Okay, browsing back to Monday, here's the first Twit from Elinor@ Sense and her relationship status is listed as "single."

Then, on Wednesday, the plot thickens. She adds this @Edward1811 fellow as a friend, and I think they're direct messaging. Only to then get interrupted on Friday with the alert that Elinor@Sense has changed her relationship status to "It's Complicated." Their walls are closed to one another.

But on Sunday, the ultimate Twit does come through. @Edward1811 updates his profile three times in quick succession, going from "Engaged," briefly to "Single," and then back to "Engaged." Elinor turns off her privacy settings and reveals her status as "In a Relationship." What an ending.

Love found. Lost. Won again. And I think I'm up to date on everybody's status at the end. I don't think I missed anything. Did I miss anything?

Don't Cross the Streams

The other day, I was on the cellphone with a co-worker talking about an upcoming project. Right as we finished, he said, "Hey, could you e-mail to remind me what we just talked about?"

I hate it when people try to cross the streams. Please don't start a conversation in one stream, like a cellphone, and then expect me to suddenly switch the conversation to a different stream, like e-mail or texting or Facebook or whatever.

I follow a simple rule: Keep the stream flowing in the channel where it started. I've asked people questions in phone messages and, hours or even days later, they've texted me back a one-word "OK" without the faintest hint of context. When you cross the streams, I lose your trail.

Call me old-fashioned. Literally. Call me back on my old-fashioned phone if that's how I've contacted you.

And don't go texting me five seconds later to ask if I got the phone message. GTPM, or whatever "got the phone message" is in texting speak. Because I haven't, or I'd have called you. WTF. What are you Texting For?

In olden times, if someone sent you a smoke signal you'd be obliged to reply with a smoke signal, not a carrier pigeon. How's a pigeon supposed to fly right with all that smoke around?

Nowadays, many people seem to think that by crossing the streams they're communicating faster and better. Here's another just-in-time update to the umpteenth change in plan. Well, I can't cross-check four devices to see if a gathering I got phoned about has later been bumped via Facebook. My regrets, air traffic control.

Over the holidays, my friend e-mailed me about a karaoke party on New Year's Eve. I'm not ashamed to admit it. I'm 38. Forwarded e-mails about karaoke are about as close as I'm going to get to a flash mob.

But when I got there his windows were dark. Something strange in the neighbourhood, I hummed to myself, without benefit of an instrumental track.

I checked my phone, and, sure enough, there's a text I missed from an half-hour ago. "No NYE Karaoke 2NTE." After solving the cryptoquote, I realized I was SOL for New Year's Eve.

I texted back, "You sick?" Which actually sent as "You suck," because I had mittens on and the automatic word guesser jumped the gun.

But you know what? It did suck. Well said, vowel-challenged word guesser.

I think I'm going to call him and voice my disappointment. Because a phone call is more serious than an e-mail, I think, in this paper-rock-scissors world of crossed streams.

What I'd really like to do is bombard him with mobile tweets. That is, release a couple carrier pigeons in his car. Those streams would send a message, olden-times-style.

The Order of Canada

I'm in favour of the Order of Canada. But I'm biased. I'm from PEI, and I support anything that results in free plane rides to Ottawa.

What is the Order of Canada? At the Olympics, usually fourth.

So as a country, we came up with the perfect "Own the Podium" program. The Order of Canada. Where we actually own the podium and only let a few honorary non-Canadians get up on top of it.

The Order of Canada honours that rarest of things: the famous Canadian. That's a contradiction in terms, like "The Quiet American."

Other than the Order, the TV show *Front Page Challenge* was the longest-running attempt to celebrate Canadian achievement. The show's panellists used questions to try to identify a mystery guest.

Even *after* the mystery guest got revealed, the big question stayed the same — "Who the hell is that?"

Canadians are front-page-challenged. And the Order of Canada does the good work of trying to protect the rare birds of Canadian renown.

We need it because we're not a nation of conquering generals, we're a nation of peacekeepers. Peacekeepers are like bee-keepers — there's a special helmet, but in case of a real attack you better run like everybody else.

The Order of Canada honours our style of winners, who eventually lose and get fired, like Scotty Bowman or Paul Martin. Both recently inducted to the Order for creating jobs for Canadians — in Detroit.

The Order hasn't even kicked out Conrad Black despite him surrendering citizenship for the House of Lords and going to U.S. prison.

The Order of Canada is bigger than British parliament and American jails. It probably even protected Black while he was in prison. Because U.S. inmates wouldn't touch anyone whose gang bling is that weird-looking.

What would happen in jail if Conrad Black wore a powdered wig and told everybody he was from the House of Lords? My guess is that he would become a companion, and not of the Order of Canada.

Finally, the Order of Canada ceremony is a great way to repatriate our few famous citizens, who live in the United States. You try getting Ryan Gosling up here to be in a depressing Canadian movie about incest and schoolbus crashes.

And our stars might even stay after receiving the Order. Good luck flying back into the United States with an obscure chunk of metal strapped to your body.

I lived in the States. An airport cavity search is the only free public healthcare you'll ever get down there. If that doesn't make you respect the Order of Canada, I don't know what will.

PEI Voter Turnout

Prince Edward Island is a spot where almost everyone marks an "X."

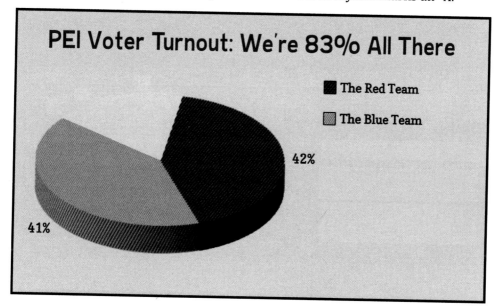

We have the highest voter turnout in the country, a percentage floating around 83% for provincial elections. Some vote for the Red Team, others for the Blue Team. But most Islanders vote early and often. By which I mean, at every electoral opportunity.

But it's surprising voter turnout isn't higher given the network of services that Red and Blue Teams extend to haul Island voters to the polls. Are you housebound, without a car? You'll be called and offered a drive.

Just chillaxing in an apartment with your 18-year-old friends, playing some video games? How about a pizza by special delivery? Where you all hop in this van first, take a pit-stop by the polling station, and then get delivered back home with a pizza?

Assisting the old and infirm and the young and the restless, these support teams fan out across the Island landscape on election day and try to locate every single voting-age Islander with two feet and a heartbeat.

If you can fog a glass and mark an "X," get in the van.

All this begs an obvious question. The election-day personhunt unearths 83% of voting Islanders. Who are the 17% that somehow slip under the province-wide radar? What could so immobilize an Islander that they are either unfindable — or unmovable — by the voter-sniffing teams?

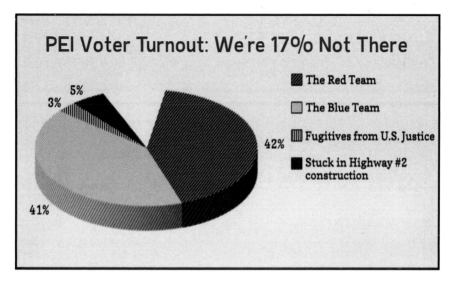

As you can see above, one block of non-voting Islanders is made up of fugitives from American justice. They are actively trying to disappear off the map, which is why they fled to PEI, a place known for being cartographically missing.

Why else do you think they bought that drafty overpriced split-level out the wharf road? Sure, they may be able to stay off the voter rolls. But someone should tell American fugitives that the Island is the worst place on Earth to avoid detection by your neighbours, due to a combination of raccoon-like curiosity, winter unemployment, and satellite-delivered American Justice TV.

Another block of non-voting Islanders is stuck in Highway #2 construction. And have been since the summer, just west of the Blueshank Road. They will not be reaching the polls anytime soon. Or home, for that matter.

Many people living in the town of Kensington were originally trying to get from Summerside to Charlottetown. They got stuck in Highway #2 construction, gave up, resettled, and had new families.

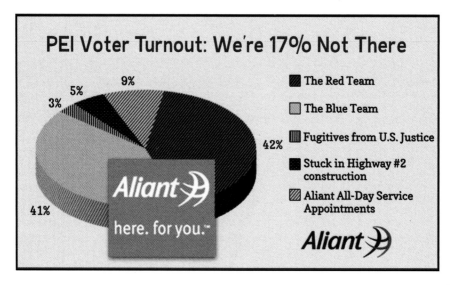

The final block of non-voting Islanders is stuck in their homes waiting for Bell Aliant all-day service appointments. They cannot leave the house to vote on election day. Not between 8:00 AM and 6:00 PM, anyway, which is when the phone repairperson may show up.

Politicians come and politicians go. If the phone company comes, and you're gallivanting off to vote or something, they won't be back for a long while. Call and press pound all you like. Hello, your phone isn't working.

Instead of voting, you are in for a full day standing by the window with the curtains slightly parted, muttering, "I am here. For you. All the livelong day."

An all-day appointment is not really an appointment. It's a form of house arrest.

CONSULT
YOUR DOCTOR

Being Celiac

When my doctor broke the news that I'm a celiac, two questions flashed in my brainpan. The first was "Oh no, whatever will become of me?" And the second was "What is a celiac?"

Clearly some kind of maniac, I know, but what kind?

My doctor went on to explain that being celiac means I'm gluten intolerant. Well, thanks for clearing that up Dr. Master Communicator. What the heck is *gluten*?

Time to head home for some Internet self-diagnosis.

If I were to oversimplify what I learned on the Internet, then gluten is the wheat protein that makes bread elastic. Gluten is what puts the spring in your baguette, the chewy in your bagel.

And like roughly 2% of the population, my gastrointestinal tract just doesn't absorb gluten. In fact, I'm rubber, and it's gluten. Whatever bread I eat bounces off my insides and sticks to you.

This explains a lot.

Like why my experience running a marathon a couple of years back turned into such a movie-of-the-week. In hindsight, I suppose carbing up with four Everything bagels that morning wasn't the best strategy ever.

I armed myself with a ticking bread bomb, and then rumbled off for a 42-kilometre run. And, like the bagel name predicted, everything happened. I visited all port-a-potties. My Chariots of Fire, I dubbed them.

Life's been a whole lot less rumbly since I switched to a gluten-free diet, although it's a huge change. I had a long love affair with bread, ripping through extra slices like some people go through paper towels. Bread was the best thing since... basically ever.

Sure, there are more gluten-free options available from the local grocer. If you really want to know what gluten is, try some of these gluten-free products and taste what's not there. Mainly, moisture and affordability.

Mmmm, who makes this corn bread? Dr. Scholl's? Love that pumice-stone texture. And only $12 a loaf? Crazy, I'll take three.

The biggest drawback? Those who are intolerant of the gluten intolerant, especially at get-togethers. I say "get-togethers" on purpose because if I called these events "parties," you'd get the impression that they're fun.

I prefer not to mention my intestine at get-togethers. Because even when I explain celiac disease some people then act like they can just talk me out of it.

"I bet if you just exposed yourself to wheat more you wouldn't be so intolerant. Expose yourself to this sausage roll. Ha ha."

Gluten intolerance is not like racial intolerance. It won't be healed by my spending more time with gluten and realizing that we're all the same, deep down.

I'm actually a bit clinically different, deep down. Which means that crackers are my Kryptonite, and no, I would not like some of your tasty party poison, please.

"Hey, have some popcorn shrimp. What's the worst that could happen?"

Well, probably a barf on your new area rug equivalent to the amount I ate. That would probably be the worst, to answer your question.

So to the gluten-intolerant intolerant, a simple request. Don't go getting up in our faces with your dreaded, breaded treats. Leave us in peace with our rice cakes, the last truly universal snack that is nut-free, lactose-free, gluten-free, and completely flavour-free.

God, rice cakes are the last thing on earth that deserve to be called cakes.

But I will eventually build up enough saliva to swallow this rice-based packing material. And then, I will dry-mouth a thank you for making them available at your get-together.

Because I'm a celiac. And I'm not ready to rumble. In my tummy. Anymore.

Cold-Treatment Alternatives

I just dragged myself through a week with this year's seasonal flu.

Whatever it was, H2N3 or R2D2 or C3PO, it deserved a vanity plate out of *Star Wars* because it attacked my system like a robot from outer space.

Sorry to be so dramatic. When I get sick, I go a bit Hollywood. Red-eyed and house-arrested like a tarnished celebrity, with a dedicated team of bottled products overseeing my recovery.

At the pharmacy these days, there's such a dizzying array of possible treatments available. Over-the-counter cold medication, naturopathic and vitamin alternatives, and even traditional remedies like honey, lemon, and denial.

It can be hard to know your treatment options and choose among them. But not for me. I just take them all, inconsistently and at different times, and let them talk out their differences among themselves.

For starters, I probably have unreasonably high expectations of brand medicines. I blame their crime-fighter names. Benadryl. Advil. Robitussin.

After taking these medications, I imagine them flying through my body on a forensic mission, as clean and targetted as effects sequences on *CSI*. Dodging red blood cells big as throw-pillows and shooting spidery viruses with surgical-strike lasers.

In my experience, cold medication travels through my body less like *CSI* and more like *Matlock*. Benadryl Matlock, Attorney at Law. The medication bumbles around for about an hour, talking to all organs, even if not connected with the crime.

"Hey, I'm the bowels. Nice to meet you, too, Ben. Nope, I haven't seen the flu anywhere. But maybe you can hop aboard and we'll look around together.

"Hey, did anyone ever tell you, you put people immediately at ease?"

To balance things out, I add naturopathic remedies to the conversational mix. Like a celebrity who retains a private detective, but also a spiritual advisor. Just to feel secure and covered on all possible fronts.

"*Namaste*, everyone. My name is Echinacea Garlicpills. Yes, my parents followed the Grateful Dead. How did you guess?

"Don't mind me, I'm just scattering some Purple Coneflower around this immune system to restore the aura. Don't ask me how it works — it just does."

Finally, my grandmother's home remedies enter into the conversation of conflicting medical advice, which by now is getting loud.

"Try hot toddies with honey, butter, and rum. But don't drink too many, or you'll get your hangover mixed up with your cold symptoms.

"If you're still not better after a day or two, take a spoonful of sugar with a couple of drops of kerosene oil." That way, we can burn your body when you pass away.

"Now stop playing the martyr and get some rest."

Right before my fever broke, I had a dream as peaceful and strange as afternoon TV. A spiritual advisor fixed up a blind date between my grandmother and Ben Matlock, who brought some purple coneflowers and took her out for dinner by old-fashioned lamplight.

"Maybe I shouldn't even be talking to you while working on your grandson's case. Oh, by the way, he's not dying," said Matlock with garlic-laden breath.

"I already told him that," said Grandma, hoisting aloft another tumbler of rum. "Did anyone ever tell you that you put people immediately at ease?"

Winter Preparedness

It's time for another episode of "Ask Patrick." Hard questions, real answers. Today's topic is "How to Survive a PEI Winter."

If you want to stay healthy and happy until spring arrives on the Island (somewhere around mid-June), you're going to have to make real lifestyle changes.

Q: *My wife bought me a fashionable Thinsulate jacket for Christmas. She loves how it looks on me. It's rated up to -40 degrees, but I'm freezing. What should I do?*

A: Reality check time. Let's face the thermodynamic laws of an Island winter. The warmth of a winter jacket is inversely proportional to its sexual attractiveness. Explain to your wife that a good winter coat repels the windchill and members of the opposite sex. It has to do both.

Q: *Do you have any suggestions for a good wind-breaker?*

A: If you wear a wind-breaker in a PEI winter you'll inflate like a driver's-side air bag. I warn you. Roll up that breathable K-way and stick it back in its pocket until spring. Unless you want to store your ears in that pocket too, after they freeze and fall off.

Q: *I'm originally from PEI, but we're having a real tough winter in Vancouver. What should I do when I'm on my bike and my Birkenstocks are getting damp and...*

Sorry, Vancouver. Wrong Island. Open-toed footwear is not relevant to PEI winter survival. So, put a sock in it.

Q: *Everybody says dress in layers. How do I know when to stop layering?*

A: Before stepping out the door, I like to give myself a pat-down test. If I can feel enough through my layered clothing to identify my own gender, I go back and put on more layers until I'm asexual and ready for a day outside.

Am I coming through loud and clear? If not, I hope it's because you're already zipped deep into a periscope-shaped hood and can't hear anything but the rush of blood through your own brain.

Stay right there until spring.

We Don't Quit on Things

As Islanders, we don't quit on things. We have a talent for taking other people's trash. Actually *taking* it, often under cover of darkness. And we somehow manage to transform that trash into our lasting treasure.

For example, who was first pushed in that baby carriage? Moses?

This talent for making things last longer is nothing new.

My grandmother was the original queen of seeing the good left in things. She washed plastic wrap and hung it out on the line to dry.

The only problem? Plastic wrap's transparent. So the neighbours would be peeking across the fence and thinking that she was hanging out nothing. And that maybe grandma was one sock light of a load.

But grandma had the last laugh. She got four uses out of every sheet, especially if the next batches of banana bread all came out the same size.

Tourists ask us questions. Questions like, how can Islanders afford to have a cottage that's only 15 minutes from the house? It's easy. Because we decorate our cottages with garbage. Good garbage, though, saved with art and imagination.

Say you're driving around in the springtime, and you spot a tire lying in the ditch, full of rainwater, breeding mosquitoes. Many North Americans would drive on past that tire, making remarks like, "That's an environmental hazard. That's a shame."

Islanders don't drive past. We stop the car and send one of the kids from the backseat to grab that tire and put it in the trunk. Because we look at the tire, and we consider the lawn at the cottage, and then look back at the tire.

And in our imaginations, this tire is magically transformed into a possible flowerbed. Full of steel-belted begonias.

These flowerbeds are an ideal arrangement. There's nothing better after a hard week's work than climbing on the ride-on lawnmower and then just ripping around the yard, waling into your flowerbeds. And you won't shake a petal because those flowers are steel-belt protected against the likes of you.

There're all kinds of things that Islanders can spy, with our little eyes. For instance, a purple toilet destined for the landfill. Hey, get that off the back of the half-ton! That's a perfectly good broken toilet, and I could use that for something.

My father saved our freshly uprooted 1970s purple toilet. He plunked it out in the middle of the yard, and he planted it full of chives. He pumped in the topsoil, and the toilet pumped out the chives, all summer long.

If you're visiting the province, don't leave before you have some new potatoes sprinkled with some toilet chives. It's a distinctive regional flavour, and you'll be a long time shaking it.

Build more drawers in your house now because you're going to need them. Extra drawers to store buttons without shirts, zippers whose jeans are long gone, and little bits of yellow rope.

What are you doing throwing that yellow rope in the black waste cart? That's ten inches of perfectly good rope. I'm going to use it.

Because if you have ten inches of good yellow rope and a bit of paint and a bit of plywood, you're well on your way to a masterpiece of lawn art.

Spilling over with irrepressible mischief of youth, serving notice to locals and visitors alike that everybody can let their guard down. It's an unmistakable welcome to our province. I look at this art, and I immediately think, "Urine PEI."

We've all experienced that awkward moment at yard sales when we see a busted Barbie, once a loved companion, now abandoned. Her hairdo askew, her heart broken by that faker Ken and his empty plastic head and his camper full of lies.

As Islanders, we're called to help restore her self-esteem.

We give her a makeover and a new role in essential bathroom handicraft.

Upper torso Barbie, lower torso crochet skirt to hide the spare roll of toilet paper from the houseguests, in case they need it.

If some of your guests can't find the spare roll in this arrangement, they'll have to use an old *Chatelaine* magazine. Figure it out.

Here, you might see nothing but a rusted-out 1990 Pontiac Sunbird fit for the wreckers. I see a pleasure craft that's ideal for the one summer left in it.

Inspection? No problem. I'll take it to a country mechanic and leave Captain Morgan on the dash to point out where the inspection sticker needs to go. Avast, me hearty inspector. Stick 'er right there.

It's got no turn signals? No problem. I only go four places. You'd think people could pick up on a pattern. It's got a bit of play in the steering column, so the Sunbird is sexually attracted to the ditch? Not to worry. I'm only driving it on the red dirt roads, where the ditches are so soft that they practically embrace you on the way in.

That's how you stretch your car's life longer on PEI. First, you stop driving it on the main highways. Then, you stop driving it on the paved secondary roads. Then, you're left sneaking around on the red dirt roads, avoiding the cops.

Until the rust starts to creep up your rocker panels like the red dirt road is coming to reclaim your car. To iron oxide, everything returns.

So, for this last summer, you better drive that car.

You better drive it until the smoke curls up from around the hood, until the wheels catch fire and melt off. Until you're ready to take the

Sunbird down a red Island road for the last time, straight into the evening sky, and have it go out in a blaze of glory.

Quit on that car?

We're Islanders, and we do not quit on things.

BETTER HOMES AND GUARDRAILS

Having a Yard Sale

I'm having a yard sale. But it looks like a home eviction with masking-tape price tags.

Friends, neighbours: Slow down your cars and come pick through the train wreck.

No, sir, that desk isn't oak. Unless it's oak that's been ground up like hamburger and then laminated with fake plastic oak. Did you fall off the *Antiques Roadshow* and land on your head?

Sorry, madame, I do not still have the warranty for that ancient toaster. Stick a fondue skewer in it and see if it works.

I do have some better things on display to maintain the one-letter distinction between "garage sale" and "garbage sale." But the saleable items aren't any less painful for me to cart out.

Because a yard sale is like being forced to watch a blooper reel of your most poorly thought-out purchases. These things embody entire attitudes towards life that I tried on for embarrassingly short periods of time. I'm not just trying to get rid of stuff. I'm saying goodbye to the hoped-for versions of myself that these products represent.

Goodbye, big purple exercise ball. I will never have the rock-hard abs that you represent. Because even with your awesome back support, 500 crunches are not going to be part of my morning. Unless 500 crunches is a breakfast cereal.

I cannot have you in the house pulsing like a cheap prop in a *Star Trek* episode where an orb-like parasite feeds off the resentments of the crew. I accept that my hopes — and midsection — have become as slightly deflated as you, exercise ball with the slow leak somewhere.

Oh, nameless lady in the yoga pants, what price will make you take this talisman of failure from my sight, without revealing my desperation to be rid of it?

And farewell, handmade pasta-machine version of myself. I recognize I am no more likely to hand-make pasta than I am to hand-make paper towels. I do not know what I was thinking when I bought a machine that takes something convenient and cheap and makes it difficult and time-consuming.

I accept I will never spend hours in the kitchen cranking out pillowy angel-hair pasta with one arm. Shirtless and singing in Italian, olive oil rippling off my Renaissance abs, produced by the purple exercise ball I mentioned earlier.

Oh, bourgeois bohemian couple, how can I sing the praises of this device and convince you to remove it from the property forever?

My life junk is taking wing, and I can see new plans taking flight with it.

If you don't believe hope springs eternal, have a yard sale. It'll show you that, like an exercise ball, hope does deflate but only to a certain point.

I feel lighter already.

Do Not Drink-and-Dial List

Are you bothered by pesky calls from telemarketers? "Yaharr, matey! You may have won a pirate cruise in the Capt'n Ahoy Sweepstakes."

I used to get upset because I didn't like the interruptions, and I didn't like the surly person I became.

"Blow it out your porthole, you son of a biscuit eater!"

But my phone life has improved since the creation of the national Do Not Call List. Signing up was easy. And now, my number is in a no-call registry that all telemarketers have to check and observe. Yo ho ho, scurvy pirate cruise offers, and avast with ye.

But the list has not cured all my phone-related ills. It takes care of annoying *incoming* calls. But what about the ill-advised *outgoing* calls I sometimes make? The sloppy after-hours calls, when my blurry judgment is not making good phone decisions.

Building on the success of the Do Not Call List, I propose that Canada launch a national Do Not Drink-and-Dial List. Here's how it would work. While sober, I call in to register a personalized list of numbers that I should not — under any circumstances — be allowed to call between midnight and 8:00 AM.

My college drinking buddy, now with the infant twins. My long-past ex, who left for a West Coast timezone on pretty bad terms. I know she took my favourite T-shirt, but calling her ten years later at 4:00 AM, isn't really going to get that shirt back now, is it?

Let's explore a Do Not Drink-and-Dial scenario. Say I'm up late on a Wednesday night, enjoying a few nightcaps, revisiting my decision to move from college teaching to comedy writing. Yeah, I gave up dental benefits. What was the sense of having dental when no one on staff ever felt like smiling? Explain to me that.

Say I get the notion to give a ring-a-ding to my former supervisor right then and there to elaborate on my reasons for leaving.

Like how it sucked answering e-mails in the early hours of the morning. And how at least now, at 2:00 AM, I get to call *real* people up, you know, and talk about what *really* matters, you know.

If there were a Do Not Drink-and-Dial List, I'd have the foresight to enter all former bosses' home numbers on my no-call list. So a call like this one would be blocked, and a friendly-but-firm message would bring me to my senses.

"Hello. This number is on your Do Not Drink-and-Dial List, and cannot be reached at 2:00 AM, in your frame of mind. Please call back when your blood alcohol reaches point-zero-eight or 8:00 AM, whichever comes first."

Yes, I'd probably curse this system like a pirate, by night.

But I'd much prefer to be shackled by this system than to waken to an ominous red message light the next morning. Yaharr, sailors take warning!

Contradictory Sport Combinations

What is it about the Winter Olympics that makes me totally lose my mind?

Two weeks before the Olympics start, I couldn't give a triple Salchow for whatever's happening in the figure-skating world. But as soon as the Olympics arrive, I perform a full 360-degree rotation. My heart leaps in my chest whenever our Canadian pairs attempt a triple Lutz twist lift. I don't even know what that means.

When I analyze it, I'm most drawn to the Olympic sports that pull together unrelated and even contradictory skill sets. Like figure skating. Artistry and force. Strength and grace. Wearing fancy outfits, and then trying to jump higher than you can consistently manage, even in practice.

What other life activity asks people to first dress up in formalwear, and a little later, sprawl all over the place? In Atlantic Canada that's called a wedding, and trust me, it's hard on everybody.

I respect figure skaters. You would never go to the ballet and see dancers try leaps that risk turning tutus into Swiffers, wiping out into the orchestra pit. Well, I never go to the ballet, period. But I might, if ballet dancers put as much on the line as figure skaters.

Or biathletes. Talk about your activities rigged to fail. In biathlon, one half of the sport gradually ruins the athlete's ability to do the other half of the sport. First, let's get you skiing until your heart is pounding like a jackhammer. And now let's try shooting this target the size of a jackrabbit's left nut.

I respect biathletes. I know who I want in my corner if Canada is ever invaded in winter immediately after a heavy snowfall but before the tanks and planes have been plowed out.

The mind-boggling contradictions of biathlon make other sports seem humdrum. It's like boxing but then having to read an eye chart between rounds. Can't pick out the bottom row? Sorry, that's going to mean some demerit points. Try not getting hit in the face so much.

That wouldn't seem fair. But that's just it. There's drama in athletes being thrust into a contradictory world that's stopped making sense. And we recognize our own fight against futility in their stronger, higher outlines.

Who hasn't felt like a figure skater, all dressed up with nowhere to go but down? And who hasn't felt like a biathlete, given two unrelated things to do that don't help each other in the least?

So that's why I'm awake and glued to the set, watching the Canadian athletes who represent us. I want them to emerge triumphant from their years of obscure toil and to wrestle victory straight out of the jaws of contradiction.

Whose heart wouldn't glow at the sight of that?

Under the
Acadian Influence

At a glance, you may not realize the influence of Acadian francophone culture on PEI. But every time you're at a Gallant's, you're experiencing that influence. Look at the phone book under Rustico — it's basically Gallants.

It's a complex history. Fortunately, I have six years of French in the PEI public school system. So I'm very well qualified to explain Acadian culture to you with 38 words of French vocabulary.

"*Je m'appelle Patrick. J'aime les flocons de maïs pour le petit déjeuner.*" Let's give this a try. *On y va.*

The Acadian influence is all over the map in the Island's community names.

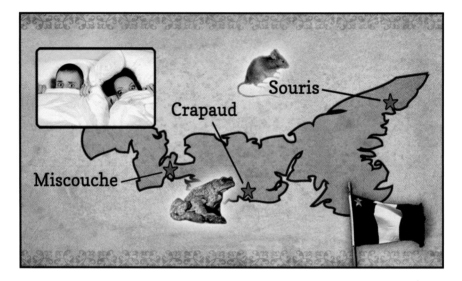

To the East, the community of Souris. As an English-speaking Islander, I pronounce these syllables entirely through my right nostril. Very harsh-sounding: Siir-eee.

It's actually a French word with far more romance than we give it credit. "Souris" means "mouse." Not a super-fun time for the early French settlers up there, by the sounds of things.

"Are we staying here, Sieur Robert, with the rodent outbreak? No Siir-eee, Bob! *On y va!*"

Towards the centre of the province, it's lovely Crapaud. Stop laughing, it's not what it seems. In French, "crapaud" actually means "toad." Okay, maybe not much better than what the English sounds like.

To the West, we find ourselves in Miscouche. Which in English means "In bed with the wrong person." You know, like the popular disco hit, "*Voulez-vous couchez avec moi, ce soir?*"

If you fall easily for Acadian lines, with all that sweet "*voulez-vous,*" you better watch yourself up there in that bedroom community. The Acadian people are very welcoming, and they have perfect teeth. Things can happen.

"*Ah zut, j'ai miscouché encore. Au revoir! Je suis très, très désolé.*"

"*Maudit espèce de crapaud!*"

Our bus company with fast service out of PEI is called Acadian Lines. Let that serve as a warning to you.

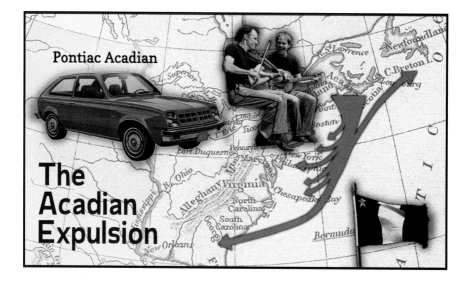

The Acadians weathered many plagues. Mice, toads, and the worst plague of all, the British, who tried to deport the Acadians from the Atlantic region in the late 1700s. Probably because the British hate anyone with a good sense of rhythm. And good teeth.

Never dance or smile around the British. They will expulse you.

The Acadians were left stranded on the road, all over North America. It's this history of unwelcome travel which General Motors marked in 1978, with the Pontiac Acadian. A car which also left people stranded on the road all over North America.

But between those Acadians who stayed and those who returned, the Acadian influence is everywhere. Because they create art from everything they touch. Nothing in the house goes undecorated.

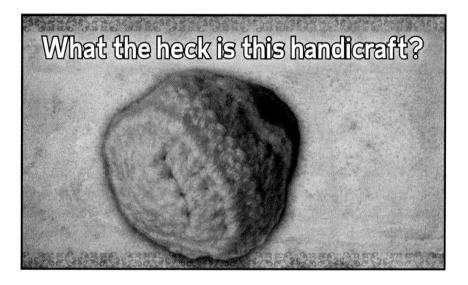

When my wife and I got married, we were lucky enough to receive four of these Acadian handicrafts as a wedding present. I remember plucking them out of the tissue paper at our gift opening, surrounded by watching relatives.

Four yarn pockets in a box. My face was paralyzed in a Botox death-mask of surprise. I was so at a loss for words to express my thanks.

Because I had no idea what to call the four little yarn pockets. Baptismal booties for the dog?

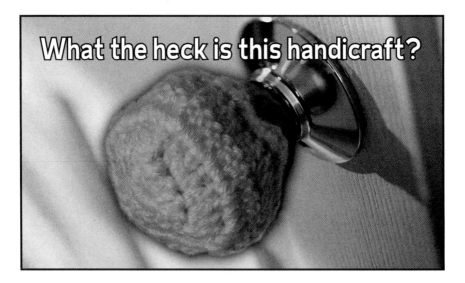

No, you can obviously see what these are. These are Acadian hand-hooked doorknob covers. How could I have missed that? I felt like such an *espèce d'idiot*.

I shamefully realized that, for years, my homes have been nudist colonies of naked knobs. Sticking out at people, all protruding and brassy. What must the neighbours have been saying?

It is much better now that I'm married. With our doorknobs at home securely covered in Acadian handicraft, the doors are impossible to open. I just stand there for a couple of minutes, polishing the knob, until I decide that I don't want to go into that room anyway.

There was a point in my life when popping out for half-a-dozen knob covers would have meant something radically different.

Now I can't even open the front door.

But plus ça change, plus c'est la même chose. Roughly translated from the French: change happens, life stays the same.

And if you can't deal with that, good luck sticking around as long — and shining as bright — as *mes amis* the Acadians.

HETERO-SCHEDULED

Valentines Underwear

This Valentine's Day, I'm playing it safe and sticking with chocolates. The fancy kind, individually wrapped, so my wife and I walk on a romantic carpet of gold foil as we eat them going upstairs.

In the past, I've tried more adventurous ways of showing my wife how much I love her. I've bought special articles of, you know, underwear.

In the shop, I snapped up the shiniest and dangliest things I could find, like an impulsive, unknowing trout. Going for it. Hooks, lace, and slinky.

But in a committed relationship, I've noticed an interesting thing about special underwear. It works its way into your partner's daily rotation. Bras are expensive, my wife says. So if, as a spouse, you spring for one that's silky and halfways structurally sound, expect to see it again regularly, and not for your benefit.

It's no longer just a ninth-inning closer. It's on the schedule, called on to start every sixth or seventh day. And it's in the dryer, its tender hooks tangled with the sweat socks of everyday life.

I know this intricate scenario firsthand because I share in the folding at our house. I fold. Not only in arguments, but those as well.

And I've needed to develop innovative approaches to folding the special underwear from Valentine's days past.

First, the bra. I don't wear one, except on Hallowe'en just about every year. But I figured the bra out. Fellows, it's hinged in the middle. Close the cups of the bra on each other like a burger bun and then set the closed bun to the side. Imagine you're working the grill at a ball-team fundraiser on a Saturday morning.

Sometimes, I secure the bra bun, wrapping it a couple times around with the shoulder straps. And then set it aside. Home safe.

Panties are much trickier. They're so insubstantial, and so slippery.

Trying to fold panties is like trying to do origami with a candybar wrapper. I tried bunching up panties in my fists, to compact them. But they kept slowly opening right back up like panty blossoms in springtime.

Another time, I tried rolling them into one big, long panty roll, similar to the plastic bags next to the vegetables at the supermarket. Just tear fresh ones off the outside, as required. But the panties refused to roll flat, and they tangled up tighter than elastics in office drawers.

After much trial and error, I finally arrived at the best practice for folding these special items. Take a bra, open it like a burger bun, pop in a pair of panties, and then close it up. Set it aside. Keep the burger line moving.

I call it the McB'n'P. The McBra and Panties. A full day's underwearing, in one convenient grab-and-go package. It's how I show I care.

I'm inspired by how special underwear of Valentines past has folded itself into our regular lives. The articles arrived here with no more than a short-term romantic plan, not stretching past Valentine's night.

But they've proven to be strong, comfortable, and a lasting support for everyday living.

Now if only I can stretch to be all those things to my wife, too. Then, I'll have earned my spot in the permanent line-up.

New Yoga Resolution

New Year's resolution: I'm taking a yoga class with my wife.

So here I sit, waiting for our first class to start, in a bogus half-lotus, my hips artificially jacked into position by little foam pillows.

I'm supposed to be settling my mind. But there are more yoga fears dancing around my head than Vishnu has arms.

> *Yoga fact: The word "Yoga" means*
> *"to yoke together" in Sanskrit.*

And the word Patrick means "put together like a picnic table" in Gaelic. Look it up. My ancestors were Catholic potato-pickers. Don't even start with me about inflexibility.

> *Yoga fact: A popular beginning pose is the*
> *Happy Baby Pose, or Ananda Balasana.*

Funny you say that. The last time I successfully touched my toes was at three months. Happy times. The last time I tried touching my toes in public was in junior-high gymnastics. Bad times. That pose was called Gympants and Shame.

Yoga fact: Chakras are centres
in the body that transmit energy.

Well, I've located a chakra. Transmitting the message that this mat does not have enough padding for my sacral regions.

Yoga fact: Yoga uses exercise, breathing,
and meditation to create relaxation
and relieve everyday stress.

If yoga is all about relaxation, why is no one wearing yoga pants ever relaxed?

So I accidentally used more than my fair share of little foam pillows to prop up my lotus position here. The yogapanted woman behind me just gave me this glare, like she wanted to burn a third eye right through me. Sheesh. When life gives you lulu-lemons, make lulu-lemonade.

Okay, class is starting. Time to calm my yoga fears and focus on my breathing. I'm going to close my eyes, so I don't have to focus on my blinking at the same time.

This yoga teacher actually seems pretty reasonable. She's explaining that yoga is all about creating our own relationship to the pose.

What's that, teacher? I need to push a little bit farther? But I thought everyone just needed to do their best in the given moment and... Aarrgh! Attention K-mart chakras! That move is transmitting some blue-light energy right through me now.

I *am* listening to my body — because it's shouting.

Teacher says that one of the most difficult things about yoga is letting go of the ego. These uncontrolled outbursts must be a sign that I'm really getting it.

If only now my hips would collapse as quickly as my pride.

Scrabble Squabbles

In the United Kingdom, Scrabble is now selling an updated version of their standby game. Scrabble Trickster allows proper names (like cities and celebrities), abbreviations, and even backwards spelling.

I think this stratagem spells trouble, no matter which way you look at it. You know what stratagem spells backwards? Megatarts. That's not a real word, but apparently it doesn't matter anymore in crazy upside-down Scrabble land. Take your stupid 12 points.

Tossing out the rulebook is going to do a "Brangelina" on Scrabble. By which I mean, even fun needs to follow some rules, or it gets weird real fast.

My parents had more disagreements about Scrabble than anything else. My father had a Classical education, little parts of which he remembered. Late in the game, when behind, his *modus operandi* was to wedge in broken pieces of Latin like "*quo*," "*pax*," or "*ars longa*." Mom would go *habeas corpus* on him, and they'd argue *ad nauseum* about whether "*ars*" was a valid word, and whether he was behaving like one.

We'd sometimes have to get dinner *in loco parentis*, i.e., because our parents were acting like crazy people.

That is, until the children chipped together one anniversary and bought them the official cloth-bound Scrabble dictionary. Its arrival brought a *Pax Scrabble-mana* to our household. Because there were now some rules of reference, rather than a battle to catch each other *in flagrante delicto*, outright inventing Latin words.

I avoided Scrabble for many years because I associated it with conflict. Which is too bad because the game would have been an outlet for my experience as a word-nerdy, scabby-faced adolescent.

In my teens, a dermatologist told me that my skin flare-ups were a combination of psoriasis and eczema. If I played Scrabble at the time, both those words would have been excellent scores which I would've known how to spell. Eczema! 19 points. I'd have been itching to work that one in.

Now, I'm married and my wife and I have tentatively started playing Scrabble. But I've learned my lesson: There need to be clear rules of engagement or someone's going to wind up *persona non grata*.

For example, we've established the "No Whistling" Scrabble rule. My wife is a talented whistler, but she shouldn't whistle when it's my turn.

And she shouldn't choose such incredibly difficult songs to whistle as "These Eyes" by the Guess Who.

Once, before we established the rule, she interpreted my request for silence as a musical judgment on her whistling. There was a lot of silence. I lightheartedly laid down "Cranky" as my next word and smiled, hoping to see a smile back from her now tightly pursed, non-whistling lips.

Instead, she built right down off my "C" in "Cranky," with "Celibate," getting a Double Word Score and using all her letters.

We've all picked Scrabble letters that add up to nothing but the consonant-strewn name of an Eastern European supermodel. But rather than making the rules easier, I think it's important to work with the tiles I'm dealt.

If I've nothing intelligent to add to the board maybe it's better to just skip my turn. And if I've laid out a word that doesn't correspond with reality, a simple *mea culpa* goes a long way, no matter what game you're trying to stay in.

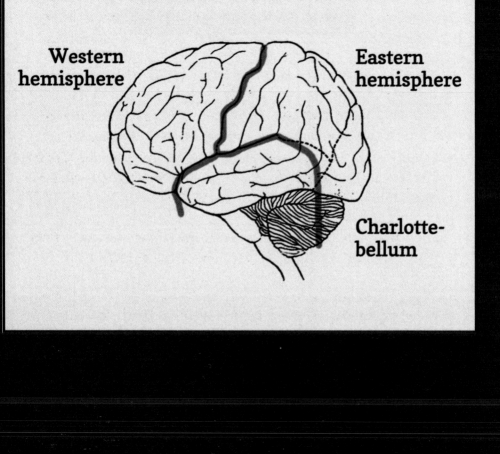

The Island mind is an object of study and ongoing fascination for mainland brain scientists.

Mainland brains have two hemispheres, the right and the left. Each hemisphere develops certain areas of specialization. The right hemisphere is better at high-school subjects like art class and emotional outbursts. The left hemisphere gets you through math and physics, and later, makes sure that the divorce papers are worded correctly.

The Island mind is even more divided.

The Island mind has two hemispheres, the Eastern and the Western. When an area of specialization pops up in one hemisphere, like a wellness centre or a Department of Education, the other hemisphere feels it needs to mirror that specialization too. Or at least something of similar size.

The end result is a pitched battle inside our own minds, where aerospace negotiations get mixed up with emotional outbursts.

In between these hemispheres sits the Charlotte-bellum, a developed and fairly dense clump. It likes to believe it is coordinating central functions. But, mainly, it gets ignored by the hemispheres.

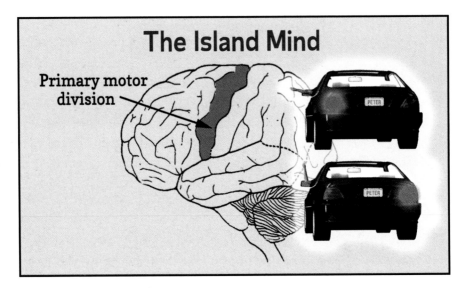

The primary motor division of the Island mind is underdeveloped and more cut off than usual from the visual and auditory senses. The Islander in motion will have huge blindspots, particularly when changing lanes. Honk away. He will remain oblivious to that stimulus, too.

In controlled lab studies, scientists have connected electrodes to the minds of Islanders to watch what is happening differently, if anything. When shown a pattern of flashing lights on the rear back right or left of a vehicle, the Island mind responds with no coordinated neural activity.

Instead, the mind gives off short firings of delight similar to what you'd expect if the subject was shown Christmas lights on a house. Which might explain why some Islanders leave these flashing signals on all the time and others save them for special occasions.

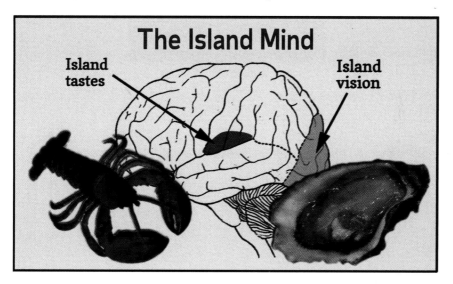

Finally, scientists have observed that taste faculties in the Island mind are located farther than usual from the visual areas. For this reason, many of our signature dishes are incredibly delicious and unspeakably ugly.

Is lobster Gaelic for "famine"? Because they look like sea spiders. Back in history, eating them must have been a desperation move.

I love lobster, but I stick to the tail and the claws. My father harangued us to pick through the questionable upper body of the lobster because "there's good eating in there." There's probably good eating in the compost bin behind the KFC, but I don't go in there either.

PEI oysters are an aphrodisiac. That figures. Because you show me someone who can forgive the snot-on-the-rocks appearance of an oyster, and I'll show you someone who can overlook your own unattractive traits.

Hey, check me out. I have hands and eyes. How'd you like a salty peck on the cheek from nature's greatest miracle?

SEASONALLY AFFECTIVE

Christmas Candy

Every Christmas, my older relatives fill up their crystal candy dishes with care, ready to pass out the old-timey holiday favourites.

Ribbon candy. Humbugs. Barley toys. What would Christmas be without this timeless Yuletide candy? I'll tell you what it would be. A whole bunch safer.

It's hard to fathom how otherwise loving grandparents still give children a candy called Chicken Bones. I have horrible memories of choking down these putrid pink shards at Grandma's house, just to be polite, as they splintered in my windpipe.

Much of this candy hasn't seen an update since the Great Depression. That was a scarcer time that forever warped our grandparents' notions of how candy is supposed to taste.

I'm sorry your first Christmases were during that harsh time, Aunt Edna. But this ribbon candy, it tastes like varnish.

More to the point, ribbon candy is dangerously pointy. When I was little and somehow managed to keep this so-called candy in my mouth for five minutes, my saliva would sharpen it into a little candy bandsaw.

Maybe Depression kids were more nimble because working in factories or on farms taught them to avoid sharp moving parts.

But giving a kid like me ribbon candy at Christmas? That's about as responsible as letting me lick chocolate pudding off a pull-top can. I learned that lesson, and so did society. Now stores no longer sell pudding with a chocolatey pizza cutter sealed on top.

Yet every Christmas there's the ribbon candy, back on the shelves waiting to scar another generation. Who will stop this holiday candy madness?

Here's a Christmas candy riddle for you. Why are these old-fashioned Christmas suckers called "barley toys"? Because a child can barley fit them into their mouths.

If you are a holiday lollipop designer, why confine yourself to shapes actually proportional to a child's face? At the barley toy factory they create elaborate sucker scenes that nestle into the cheek about as well as a collectible figurine. Oh, it's Santa's pointy sled on a pointy rooftop, with Santa's boots sticking up out of a pointy chimney.

A full afternoon of holiday fun bruising your face before that sugary statue is going to be even halfways lickable.

Some year, I'm going to track down the barley toy factory and confiscate the moulds they've been using since Dickens was in diapers.

So, sorry Aunt Edna, hold the old-timey candies this year.

And if you think I'm ruining Christmas tradition, well, a "Blech, humbugs" to you.

Getting the Tree

There's nothing like going out to cut your own Christmas tree. Gather up your tribe and go crashing through the snowy woods, snorting out frosty vapour like a tree-seeking steam engine. All you need is a crisp winter day, a hacksaw, and a relaxed attitude towards local laws.

First, we're going to locate a stand of evergreens not super-near anyone's house. We're going into the woods near the railway because that's usually Crown land. We're not likely to bump into the Queen of England, are we, skidooing around her Canadian landholdings in winter? "Wow, your Majesty. You still look just like your quarter."

Notice that the woodland ground underfoot can get boggy this time of year. To protect against cold feet, we've brought the essential equipment — a bottle of Scotch. Give me a honk off that. You can't dwell on your bog-drenched feet when you're full of Scotch. Ask the Scottish. They've built a culture around mossy liquor, wet feet, and trespassing on Crown land.

Now, we're deep in the woods and...

Heads up! My idiot brother always lets the branches lash out behind him. It's like having a Christmas wreath shot at you with a crossbow.

While we're holding the branches here, shielding our eyes, let's check the needles to suss out what kind of evergreens we're dealing with. These needles are flat and blunt-ended, so we have a fir on our hands. These needles are square when you roll them between your fingers, so it's a spruce. Um, if you sniff your fingers after rolling this needle, and smell cat urine, that's because we're dealing with a cat spruce.

You invite that thing inside, put lights on it, and get its sap flowing, and your house is going to smell like you have 24 feral cats. I kid you not. Cat pee is the smell of future loneliness. Worst Christmas ever.

Most years, we finally go with a Scotch pine… the pine that looks half-decent when the Scotch is gone. It's gone? Okay, let's hack something down.

You're going to take the saw and notch the tree in the direction you want it to fall. For example, I'm aiming this tree at my brother so he gets the faceful of branches that's been a long time coming to him.

Timber! How that's for a Christmas needle exchange?

It's time to drag our trophy out of the woods, laughing all the way, ha ha ha. How the heck did we manage to walk in this damn far, ha ha ha?

On the edge of the woods now, and we can finally get a good look. It seems we've cut down two trunks grown together, like hairbrushes, each with no bristles on one side. Oh well, we'll just turn the bare patch against the wall. We'll lash the trunks together with gold garland and cover up the mistakes with tinsel.

Natural trees are not even close to perfect — they always look fullest in the woods, all tangled up.

But I still suggest pulling your scraggly selves together and heading out to get one. It could be the Scotch talking, but this time of year we're not all that different from the trees.

We seem fuller when we're joined together, flinging the branches of the family tree in each other's faces.

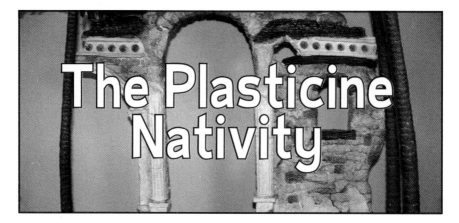

The Plasticine Nativity

Then, there was the year our family made the Christmas Nativity. Out of Plasticine. I was almost thirteen. My older sister had a year on me and the other younger siblings were spread across the spectrum, downwards from there.

The idea was touched off by watching too many claymation specials. Specials like Rudolph and Frosty, and other happy Christmas tales about being rejected by friends or melting away to nothing right after finding acceptance. The specials had gotten us pretty worked up about the possibilities of clay.

Like gambling Roman soldiers, we drew straws to divide up the usual suspects of the Nativity: shepherds and wise men, Joseph and the Virgin. We decided it was only fair to let one of the youngest make the baby Jesus.

We split up the primary colours of Plasticine and went off in our separate directions to create the Nativity figures.

When we got back together at the stable an hour or two later, it was clear we should have agreed on some common yardstick for the Biblical figures. Like how many cubits tall a baby should be as compared to a wise man, and so forth.

I made Joseph, and he was more detailed than anything in scripture. I lavished an hour's work on his beard alone. Maybe because of all that detail he turned out as a miniature.

Joseph was dwarfed by his wife Mary, created by my younger sister. Mary was blue and absolutely gigantic. Round yon Virgin, indeed. She was looking every bit the part of the Mother of God.

Her arms were bolt outright, in a gesture of either infinite forgiveness or upcoming flight.

Baby Jesus was made by the baby in the family at the time. Baby Jesus was white and had barely any details at all, as is theologically accurate, at this early stage in life.

Baby Jesus had been fashioned by that old standby of Plasticine techniques — the rolled-out log. He was a radiant beam, the kind that you could use in building a radiant barn.

He had two beady coal-black eyes that kept rolling off and getting vacuumed into the carpet.

Baby Jesus looked like a larva. Very different from the babies in Old Masters paintings, who always look almost old enough to borrow the family camel for the weekend.

There was a shortage of white clay because it had all been rolled into the Baby Jesus Yule log.

So the wise men my brothers built had bright orange or dark pink faces. These hues created the impression the kings were badly sunburnt after voyaging from country afar.

As we all know, the main way to tell a shepherd from a wise man is by the hat.

When making a wise man from Plasticine, the trick is to make the crown fancy but not too heavy. With these kings, heavy were the heads that wore the crowns. And the crowns were heavier still. The kings were uneasy and easily toppled.

Once the Plasticine Nativity was put together, I'd sneak downstairs early in the morning to do a site inspection. I'd find the baby's eyes on the carpet and press them back onto his log face before they got vacuumed.

The three kings would always fall into each other overnight. They'd form a teepee over top of the larva-like baby Jesus, like they were still trying to figure out what they were looking at after coming so far.

Our Nativity was not the most dignified-looking ever. But it's still that scene that comes to mind when I think of Christmas and of home.

Christmas comes around year after year. For all its much-advertised joys, the season can make me feel that I'm not in the best shape ever. I don't think I'm alone in that.

Years bring knocks and dents. Maybe this Christmas, someone's sick and not the right colour. Maybe I go to some party and then my eyes go black and keep sliding to the wrong place on my face. Have you ever felt like your head weighs a hundred pounds and you'd just as soon lie down?

The Plasticine Nativity reminds me that at Christmas it's all right to fall, because I'll fall into the people closest to me.

Once a year, I try to find the mindset of a mystery-seeking king. I try to let myself get led astray by stars. I try to fall in around half-formed stories and make something of them, even when all the figures are so undetailed they could mean anything.

I try to believe that when pulled together, all our hearts are misshapen but still malleable.

I Am an Islander: Epilogue

My name is Patrick. And I am still an Islander.

We're not the best at change. How many Islanders does it take to change a lightbulb? None. Because that lightbulb's probably just fine as it is.

Being an Islander is quite the proposition.

You start out on the Island. Some up West or down East. And then a lot move in town, and some have to go all the way out West just to find work.

But through all those moves, I'm always calling you up and asking when you're coming down home.

I am an Islander. I'm full of the old contradictions.

Sometimes, I spread other people's bad news. But I'm just getting the word out so I can organize the benefit.

And I have the longest goodbyes. I'll be the first to say I need to leave your party. And then stand next to your stove with my coat on for three hours, until I'm the last one there, and you're in your pyjamas.

I have a hard time with the goodbyes. I have the most belly-laughs at the wakes where my heart is aching.

I am an Islander.

Because I come from a place where we still speed up the car when we get to Borden-Carleton, like we're afraid the bridge is going to sail off without us.

I come from a place with a thousand different shades of green in the summertime. And in March, ten-thousand different shades of grey.

And I come from a place with the reddest roads this side of heaven. If I ever get to heaven, I think I may recognize the place.

My name is Patrick, and I am an Islander.

By this point, I hope you feel like one, too.

Acknowledgments

Thanks to my editor and agent, David Malahoff. I called David in 2007 and said that I was interested in doing more comedy writing. Most of my creative opportunities in the last five years, including this book, can be traced back to that first call. Especially with writing that's trying to be funny, it's invaluable to have someone with a trusted ear. David is the genuine article. I don't write much for public consumption without sending it for a round with his red pen, and you should thank him.

Thanks to my sister Jane for her clear-eyed edits on the manuscript. She has been correcting me since I was born (mostly to the good), and it was a gift to have her talents on this book project. Thanks to my brother Daniel for the cover illustration, and for creating it at various points on a concert tour across North America and Europe.

Thanks to Terrilee Bulger of Acorn Press, for agreeing to publish the book, even when the manuscript was made up of unglued enthusiasm and promises.

Thanks to CBC PEI in Charlottetown. Special thanks to Matt Rainnie, who originally invited me to create radio columns for *MainStreet* and then helped the columns get support and syndication through the

CBC Content Factory. The opportunity to write every two weeks was invaluable. *Mainstreet* host Karen Mair continued this very supportive role, and show producer Eva O'Hanley was not only a great engineer but also highly versatile as on-call voice talent.

Thanks to Richard Side, Anna Bonokoski, and Steve Patterson from CBC's *The Debaters*. I appreciate you taking a risk on an unknown entity, who wanted to try punching in *The Debaters*' weight class.

Thanks to director Wade Lynch and co-performer John Connolly for your collaboration in creating the Charlottetown Festival show Come-All-Ye. Also to my inspiring other co-performers Mark Haines, Ashley Condon, Caroline Bernard, and Chas Guay. The show not only gave me a chance to write the piece "I Am an Islander," it made me proud to say that phrase.

Thanks to Pat and Erskine Smith at the Victoria Playhouse, and to my co-performer Tanya Davis, for two wonderful runs of the stage production *The New Potato-Time Review*. The show gave me the chance to learn as a performer and to develop many of the PEI slideshow pieces in the book.

Thanks to Lorne and Françoise Elliott for creative friendship and for trusting me with a national taping on *Madly Off in All Directions*, despite my having a total of three fundraiser performances as previous credits.

Thanks to my mother-in-law Lorraine Costello, for sharing her photographic talents, and to all my Costello family.

And finally thanks to the friends, family, Islanders, and kind strangers who supported the on-line campaign to help fund *I Am an Islander*. By pre-buying the book, and other themed support packages, you've helped make it happen. This generous support was a real bridge across the final two months spent writing and editing the book. Thank you for giving me this clearer and calmer creative space.

I'd like to recognize the following people who made special contributions to support this book's creation.

THANK YOU

Andrew Boyer

Sean Casey, MP for Charlottetown

Dan Reynish and Susan Colwill

Melody and Robbie Dover, of Fresh Media

Emily and Earl Duffy

Alan and Anne MacAdam

Andrew MacPherson

David and Winkie Park

PATRONS

John and Lynn Dunphy, of Target Tours

BENEFACTORS

Tom and Beth Cullen, of Purity Dairy Ltd.

The following pieces were first broadcast by CBC Radio's Content Factory, in different form:

"Affectiliate," "All Teens Are Vampires," "Being Celiac," "Choosing the Perfect Cottage," "Cold-Treatment Alternatives," "Contradictory Sport Combinations," "Dangerous Christmas Candy," "Digital Baby Photos," "Do Not Drink-and-Dial List," "Don't Cross the Streams," "Getting the Tree," "Hand-me-downs," "Having a Gander," "Having a Yard Sale," "High School Choices," "New Yoga Resolution," "Our Heritage Names," "Scrabble Squabbles," "The Skinny on Summer," "Twitterature," "Vaguebooking," Valentines Underwear," "Why I Love Easter," "Wine Buying for the Non-Wine Buyer," "Winter Preparedness"

The following pieces were developed from topics commissioned for performance on CBC Radio's *The Debaters*:

"Anne of Green Gables v. the Potato," "Poetry Is Self-Indulgent and Irrelevant," "The Order of Canada"

All digital composite graphics designed and created by Patrick Ledwell

Cover illustration and Anne vs. Potato illustration by Daniel Ledwell www.danieledwell.com

Scenic photography by Lorraine Costello www.lorrainecostellophoto.ca